A Guide to Art Therapy Materials, Methods, and Applications

Written by a well-respected author and practitioner in the field of art therapy, *A Guide to Art Therapy Materials, Methods, and Applications* is an innovative, comprehensive text that guides readers in how to use basic to advanced art materials and methods in a wide range of clinical settings. Through the lens of both developmental stages and assessment, the book offers practical step-by-step instructions on how to incorporate these materials and methods into therapeutic work with patients of all ages and populations. In addition to such classic tools as drawing, paints, pastels, and clay, coverage of materials and special topics extends beyond the existing literature to include glass, knitting, quilting, wood burning, felting, digital applications, phototherapy, byproducts, and more. Unlike previous guides, this book specifies population benefits and contraindications for each material and technique. This research-based guide for using art materials in a safe and effective manner will be a welcome resource for students, seasoned art therapists, and mental health counselors.

Ellen G. Horovitz, PhD, LCAT, ATR-BC, E-RYT, LFYP, C-IAYT, founded the art therapy program at Nazareth College, Rochester, NY, is now Professor Emerita, and currently is in private practice. She is a licensed art therapist, yoga teacher, and certified yoga therapist. She has authored eight books, contributed numerous book chapters, and published more than 50 peer-reviewed articles. She conducts lectures and workshops internationally and her artwork is represented in numerous private collections. More information can be found at www.ellenghorovitz.com and www.yogartherapy.com.

A Guide to Art Therapy Materials, Methods, and Applications

A Practical Step-by-Step Approach

Ellen G. Horovitz

Routledge
Taylor & Francis Group
NEW YORK AND LONDON

First edition published 2018
by Routledge
711 Third Avenue, New York, NY 10017

and by Routledge
2 Park Square, Milton Park, Abingdon, Oxon, OX14 4RN

Routledge is an imprint of the Taylor & Francis Group, an informa business

Library of Congress Cataloging-in-Publication Data
Names: Horovitz, Ellen G., author.
Title: A guide to art therapy materials, methods, and applications : a practical step-by-step approach / Ellen G. Horovitz.
Description: First edition. | New York, NY ; Abingdon, Oxon : Routledge, 2017. | Includes bibliographical references and index.
Identifiers: LCCN 2017006073| ISBN 9781138209411 (hardcover : alk. paper) | ISBN 9781138209428 (pbk. : alk. paper) | ISBN 9781315457215 (e-book)
Subjects: | MESH: Art Therapy—organization & administration | Art Therapy—methods | Patient Safety | Risk Assessment | Handbooks
Classification: LCC RC489.A7 | NLM WM 34 | DDC 616.89/16560068—dc23
LC record available at https://lccn.loc.gov/2017006073

ISBN: 978-1-138-20941-1 (hbk)
ISBN: 978-1-138-20942-8 (pbk)
ISBN: 978-1-315-45721-5 (ebk)

Typeset in Baskerville
by Keystroke, Neville Lodge, Tettenhall, Wolverhampton

To Meghan DiPasquale, Esq., Tom D'Antonio, Esq., Christopher D'Angelo, MD, and Victoria Korth, MD. Thank you for making me "whole" again, in more ways than one.

Contents

About the Author

Artist Statement

I am inspired by nature, our transcendent and limited co-existence in the universe, and humor. A term I have coined in my publications is "aesthetic arrest." This is what drives me when truly inspired to create formed art. Because of my background as a licensed art therapist, certified yoga therapist, psychotherapist, and author of eight books, science constantly embeds itself in my work, whether through alchemy of materials, or how science and art plaits the brain. Art both fulfills and sustains me. Imagination is my driver and I incorporate all different media into my art pieces. My artwork has been sold both nationally and internationally and is represented in numerous private collections and galleries.

Dr. Ellen G. Horovitz, PhD, LCAT, ATR-BC, E-RYT, LFYP, C-IAYT

Photo by Eugene V. Marino, Jr.

Offerings

I have lectured and conducted workshops nationally and internationally and am available to travel to your organization or conduct personalized workshops in your studio. I am also in private practice and offer art therapy, yoga therapy, and psychotherapy as a means of communication.

To learn more about me, or my art, please visit my websites www.ellenghorovitz.com and www.yogartherapy.com or my Amazon page.

Publications

Please visit my Amazon page.

Preface

> Art proceeds by trusting in the human capacity to contain and convey its rage and its pain, and to transform residuals of violence into ethical relations via new forms of mediation that give birth to their own beauty and define them. It is to trust that we will be able to bear in compassion the unbearable, the horrible and the inhuman *in the human*. Critique is not lost in this artistic entrustment. Rather, critique becomes participatory in it.
>
> Bracha L. Ettinger, *The Matrixial Gaze* (1995)

This comprehensive handbook covers information on how to therapeutically use the most basic art materials right through to advanced media and byproducts. Everything from safety of materials is covered, including detailed step-by-step instructions to use in a clinical setting. Numerous case studies are included, as are population benefits and contraindications for each material herein. Written for the beginning to the seasoned art therapist, this handbook can be used by *all* mental health counselors as a guide for using art materials in a safe and effective manner.

Even for the advanced art therapist, the first chapter may be illuminating. Researching safety and equipment was eye opening for me as much of the information that I had thought to be true had changed. So even for the expert clinician, I highly recommend that she or he review the information in Chapter 1.

Chapter 2 sets the tone for how I work as an art therapist/yoga therapist/mental health practitioner. This chapter briefly discusses the importance of assessments, culture, belief systems, somatic issues, and holistically understanding your patient(s). (For a more thorough dive into those materials, see Horovitz, 2014.)

Chapter 3 begins by discussing how to set up your studio and deal with issues around time management, vacations, attire, clean-up, studio management, establishing rules, and etiquette for groups. For the beginning (and perhaps the more practiced) clinician, these aforementioned issues are meant to set the tone for your practice. Additionally, discussion of the most basic materials and DIY (Do It Yourself) recipes are embedded in this chapter. Case studies, population benefits, and contraindications of each material are considered in this chapter and each chapter that follows.

Chapter 4 outlines resources that I have employed. Because of my extensive art background (which preceded my education as an art therapist), I offer the reader countless ideas from analog to digital applications. Once again, numerous DIY recipes, applications, and research findings sprinkle the chapter via case studies, population benefits, and contraindications for all covered media. An exhaustive array of ideas and research is jam-packed into this chapter. And while this may be a section for the veteran art therapist, I encourage *all* readers to peruse it and utilize the ideas amassed as a springboard into your own practice and imagination. The last part of Chapter 4, which deals with digital applications and ethical issues surrounding this newer palette, discusses case studies where I have used apps in my clinical work.

Finally, Chapter 5 closes this book by presenting case studies, population benefits, and contraindications with ideas for using byproducts and recycled sources in art making. There are myriad reasons for this chapter, including the importance of being resourceful with art materials, and making a difference in the world. Modeling that to your patient(s) breeds respect and appreciation. In so doing, you are showing that you not only care for your patient but also for the world that we inhabit together.

In closing, the reader should know that throughout this book I use the word "patient" instead of "client" to define my relationship in the healing process. The reasons are multifold but may have to do with legal terms and definitions. "Client" is aptly defined as "a person or organization using the services of a lawyer or other professional person or company," whereas patient refers to "a person receiving or registered to receive medical treatment" (Dictionary.com, n.d.). While I am neither a lawyer nor a medical doctor, my alignment falls on the side of medical treatment, and so I think of my "patient" and myself as partners in this work together, co-creating toward wellness. (The old adage that "you cannot take your patient any further than you have gone yourself" is applicable here.)

The great Edith Kramer, my mentor in art therapy, used to close her personal notes to me with the following farewell, which I offer in kind to my readers: "ever art."

References

Ettinger, B. L. (1995). *The matrixial gaze.* Leeds: Feminist Arts & Histories Network.

Horovitz, E. G. (Ed.). (2014). *The art therapists' primer: A clinical guide to writing assessments, diagnosis, and treatment* (2nd Ed.). Springfield, IL: Charles C. Thomas.

Websites

Dictionary.com, "Client": www.dictionary.com/browse/client (Retrieved February 16, 2016).

Dictionary.com, "Patient": www.dictionary.com/browse/patient (Retrieved February 16, 2016).

Acknowledgments

> Crocheting . . . is an invitation to step back and breathe, to immerse yourself in the joy of creating. Each stitch is a meditation, a prayer and wish for the person you are gifting. When I crochet, each stitch is filled with loving prayers for the recipient. When we immerse ourselves in crochet or any other creative outlet, it gives us the chance to pause, to release, to let go, to embrace what is at hand, and focus on the work. I weave love, paint joy, bake compassion, stitch kindness, and give my heart when I crochet. Here, I enter a space that is gentle, soothing, restorative, and healing.
>
> Karen Armstrong (personal communication, printed with permission)

There are many factors that go into writing a book. But I always start with the people who have enabled me to cross the finish line. First and foremost, I thank my family: my husband, Jay (Gene) Marino, Jr. has championed me every step of the way; my children Kaitlyn (Darby), Bryan (Darby), Nick (Marino), and Paolo (Marino) (and soon to enfold Heather Foster) have encouraged me to keep writing, no matter how bleak the tunnel ahead; my sister, Nancy Bachrach, and brother-in-law, Orin Wechsberg, graciously sheltered my Kaitlyn during her bicoastal year; my brother, Len Horovitz, MD, and sister-in-law, Valerie Saalbach, have continued to sustain me through all of my endeavors with love, music, and humor; my mother, Maida Horovitz, who birthed me into this world and taught me the art of loving a good read; and finally my loving cats, Schlomo and Sydney, who licked, purred, and de-stressed me through the course of this writing.

The following art therapists (my art therapy family) also sustained my efforts through friendship and thoughtful feedback: the late Edith Kramer, Laurie Wilson, and Elizabeth Stone (my NYU mentors and now friends); Irene Rosner-David; Donna Betts; Judith Rubin; Linda Gantt; Michael Franklin; Patricia Isis; David Gussak; Marcia Rosal; my moon sandwich, Bruce Moon and Cathy Moon; and Martina Reiss.

Finally, my friends (also family, and listed in no particular order) are a constant well of support: Jessie Drew-Cates, Janet Root (and all of my Fiberista friends), Karen Armstrong, Janet Rock, and my (Westside) YMCA family for ministering to my health.

Numerous companies gave support so that I might provide a thorough review of their product lines and these companies are listed in the Additional Resources section. But specifically, I wish to acknowledge Melissa and Steve Zeitler (Citra Solv products) for their continuing support for all of my books since 2011, and Sarah Yan-Soucy (Pébéo) for her incredible generosity of time.

And last but not least, I wish to thank my editors at Routledge, particularly Elizabeth Graber. I am eternally grateful to the Keystroke editing team and the indispensable skill set of my premier proofreader, Ben Woolhead (of Read 'N' Right). I remain indebted to Ben as well as to the entire Routledge family; as always, I wish to thank Anna Moore, who first opened the door to my writings and accepted me into the Routledge fold.

1 Considerations on Safety and Art Materials

At the end of the day, the goals are simple: safety and security.
attributed to Jodi Rell, former governor of Connecticut

Regulation of Art Materials

When I grew up in the 1960s, safety regulations were lacking, to say the least. But times have changed. And while I still love the smell of gasoline and like toxic substances that challenge my health and safety, as an artist and therapist I need to protect my patients and/or potential consumers. Thus, it is important to have some facts on hand.

Consumer Protection

The U.S. Consumer Product Safety Commission (CPSC, an independent regulatory agency charged with protecting the public from injury or death associated with consumer products) now oversees the labeling of hazardous products. That's a tall order. The CPSC requires labeling of art materials that have the potential to cause chronic health effects under the Federal Hazardous Substances Act (FHSA) (Public Law 100-695).

Under the FHSA, an art material is defined as "any substance marketed or represented by the producer or re-packager as suitable for use in any phase of the creation of any work of visual or graphic art of any medium" (U.S. Code 1277). Children's products that meet this definition include, but are not limited to, crayons, chalk, paint sets, colored pencils, and modeling clay. Thus, the CPSC recommends that parents/guardians purchase only those products that are labeled with the statement "Conforms to ASTM D-4236" and that do not have any cautionary warnings on the label. (The ultimate guide for arts and crafts is available as a downloadable PDF and thus I will only summarize its salient points here. See USCPSC, n.d.)

Considerations When Working with Children's Arts and Crafts

Non-toxic art and craft supplies intended for children are readily available. But one should *always read the labels* and purchase only art and craft materials intended for children. For certain chemicals and exposure situations, children may be especially susceptible to the risk of injury. Since children are smaller than adults, exposures to the same amount of a chemical may result in more severe effects. Moreover, children's growing bodies, including their developing brains, nervous systems, and lungs, may make them more susceptible to chemicals than adults. Differences in metabolism may also affect children's responses to certain chemicals. All of these factors need to be taken into account when using art materials.

Children's behaviors and cognitive abilities may also influence their risk when working with art materials. Children under the age of 12 are less able to remember and follow complex steps for safety procedures, and are more impulsive, making them more likely to ignore safety precautions. Thus, adult measures need to be in place since children have a higher risk of toxic exposure than adults because they are (1) unaware of the dangers, (2) not as concerned with safety precautions as adults, and (3) often more curious and attracted to novel smells, sights, or sounds. (Much like my own attraction to gasoline as a child.) *(N.B.: Children do not have to be using the art and craft materials themselves to be affected; careless child or adult artists can accidentally expose other children to hazards. So be forewarned.)*

Thus, adults need to model safety procedures, use appropriate safety gear and measures, and carefully read cautionary labels in order to protect their younger consumers. Children need consistent reminders of safety rules; *there is no substitute for direct supervision.* (Under the FHSA, most children's products that contain a hazardous substance are banned, be they toxic, flammable, or other hazard identified in the statute. However, the Commission *may* exempt art materials that satisfy all three of the following criteria: (1) the hazardous substances are required for functional purpose, (2) the products are labeled with adequate directions and safety warnings, and (3) the materials are intended for use by children who are sufficiently mature (e.g., can read and heed such warnings – a pretty tall order for most children). Thus, I cannot emphasize enough that it is the responsibility of the art therapist to decide which products one can safely use with any population.

Types of Hazards

Mechanical Hazards: Strains, Breaks, Cuts, Crush Injuries, and Burns

Virtually any object can damage the human body. The most common injuries include cuts, scrapes, crush injuries, and burns. And because I will be covering burn survivors when discussing materials, one has to think about the psychological fallout of (for example) deciding whether or not to have lit birthday candles to celebrate a child's birthday. (This actually came up when running a burn survivors' group for children where the art therapists wanted to have a cake to celebrate one child's birthday. First, we asked the patient how he felt about having lit candles. He wanted them. Thus, we used them but with caution.)

Chemical Hazards: Inhalation, Skin Absorption, and Ingestion

Chemical exposures can occur through breathing fumes and vapors, absorption through the skin, or swallowing. Admittedly, I "point" my brushes by placing them in my mouth. (While I am aware that, over time, exposures to such chemicals may combine to damage my health, this is *not* a method that I would teach a child or an adult. Instead, I would demonstrate how to wipe the brush head at a 45-degree angle (side-to-side) in order to avoid toxicity.)

Even adults may taste art supplies or chew on drawing implements. I once had a dementia patient who tasted her paint. As a result, we supplied her with pudding and water with food coloring to avoid any hazardous results. Art therapists need to think outside of the box and continually adapt to patient needs. Back in the 1980s when I first started out as an art therapist, I was working with a quadriplegic young girl who really wanted to paint. So, I affixed a paintbrush to her headgear so that she could readily paint on paper. In time, she became so

Figure 1.1 A young quadriplegic girl painting a clay object, using her mouth to hold the paintbrush.

adept at using the paintbrush that she asked to use it by holding the handle in her mouth. While not the most sanitary decision, she had greater control over where the paint went and therefore a more successful outcome. Today, there are even mouth-painting easels; but it seems that people still use paintbrush handles directly in their mouths to control the media. (You can find videos of motorized mouth-painting easels on the internet; see for example this one at the Spinal Cord Injury Zone: www.spinalcordinjuryzone.com/videos/11880/motorised-mouth-painting-easel.)

General First Aid and Summary of Ways to Minimize Risks

Eye Exposure

1 Hold the eye(s) open with fingers and rinse immediately with water for at least five minutes. If wearing contact lenses, remove them after five minutes of washing and continue to rinse the eye(s) at least at five-minute intervals. *(N.B.: Rinse time depends on the degree of irritancy associated with a particular product.)*
2 For more advice, call the National Poison Control Center Hotline (1-800-222-1222), the nearest certified Poison Control Center, a doctor, or 911 if necessary.

Skin Exposure

1 Rinse the skin with water.
2 For more advice, call the National Poison Control Center Hotline (1-800-222-1222), the nearest certified Poison Control Center, a doctor, or 911 if necessary.

Inhalation

1 Move the person into fresh air.
2 For more advice, call the National Poison Control Center Hotline (1-800-222-1222), the nearest certified Poison Control Center, a doctor, or 911 if necessary.

If Swallowed

1 *Immediately* call the National Poison Control Center Hotline (1-800-222-1222), the nearest certified Poison Control Center, a doctor, or 911 if necessary.

Minimizing Risks

- *Know your materials.* Read warnings and labels. Take extra care when using unfamiliar products.

- *Limit exposures.* Substitute more hazardous materials with less dangerous ones. Avoid exposures to toxic materials.
- *Stay clean.* Always use protective gear, and practice good hygiene and waste disposal.
- *Clear the air.* Control dusts, filter air, add clean air, and remove fumes with proper exhausts.
- *Store materials properly.* Keep out of reach of children. Label all products.

General Information and Precautions for the Basics: Clay, Paint, and Papers

(N.B.: The following information has been adapted from the Art and Craft Safety Guide *(USCPSC, n.d.).)* For a complete listing of all art materials and handling, the author urges the reader to download the free PDF file. This is just a partial adaptation of that comprehensive brochure which has been published to protect the consumer.)

Clay/Modeling Clay

- Components may include hydrated aluminum silicates (with crystalline silica), talc, vermiculite, asbestos (a contaminant in some talc and vermiculite), kaolin, alumina, diatomaceous earth (silicon dioxide), and sand.
- Potential health effects from chronic long-term exposure to clay dust or powdered mix include skin irritation, lung diseases/infections (e.g., asbestosis, silicosis), and cancer (e.g., from asbestos).
- *Read the product label.* When possible, choose the safest materials available (e.g., those with few or no cautionary/warning labels).
- Avoid inhaling dust. Ensure appropriate ventilation or use a National Institute for Occupational Safety and Health (NIOSH)-approved toxic dust respirator.
- When possible, use premixed clays to minimize exposure to large amounts of clay dust.
- To reduce dust inhalation, do not pulverize dry clay or sand "greenware" (unbaked molded and shaped pottery). Instead, finish greenware while damp/wet.
- When cleaning, do not sweep dust. Use a wet mop, rags, and/or a vacuum with a HEPA filter system.
- Wear gloves and/or use moisturizer to prevent dry skin.
- Rest wrists frequently to avoid repetitive stress injury (e.g., carpal tunnel syndrome).

Clay Glazes

- These are mixtures of silica, fluxes, and colorants for finishing or coloring clay.

- Glazes may be toxic by inhalation, ingestion, and skin contact.
- Only use lead-free glazes or those with sodium, potassium, calcium, or magnesium fluxes. (Components may include arsenic, uranium, lead, chromium VI, lithium, beryllium, cobalt, antimony, cadmium, nickel, barium, vanadium, soda ash, potassium carbonate, feldspars, and fluorspar. Some glazes may contain solvents.)
- Use a National Institute for Occupational Safety and Health (NIOSH)-approved respirator when working with powdered glazes if you are not using premixed glazes.
- Use a wet mop, rags, or HEPA vacuum to clean up spilled powders. Do not sweep.
- Avoid spraying glazes but if you do, use a spray booth equipped with a fan that exhausts to the outside.

Painting General Information/Precautions

- The potential hazards from paints are primarily associated with some of the vehicles/solvents (e.g., aliphatic and aromatic hydrocarbons, ketones, and alcohols) and pigments (e.g., lead carbonate, chrome yellow, cobalt arsenate).
- *Read the product label.* When possible, choose the safest materials available (e.g., those with few or no cautionary/warning labels).
- Use premixed paints to avoid the inhalation of dry pigments/dyes/powders.
- Use water-based products or observe the precautions on hazard-labeled products to reduce the potential hazards from solvents.
- Close containers of paint, pigments/dyes, and solvents when not in use.
- Remove paint from the hands with vegetable or baby oil and then wash with soap and water.
- Avoid turpentine and mineral spirits. Instead, for clean-up purposes, it is highly recommended that the user try Citra Solv, a natural organic cleaner.
- Be aware of the flammability potential of solvents.

Specific Paint Materials Compounds

Caseins

- These consist of dried milk, pigments, and preservatives.
- They can be hazardous to people with asthma.

Encaustics

- These consist of a suspension of pigments and other materials in wax.
- They can be a burn hazard.

- Wax decomposition materials (e.g., acrolein, formaldehyde, pigment fumes) formed from heating or torching the wax may cause respiratory irritation.
- Minimize vapor formation by only heating the wax to the minimum temperature required for melting.
- Avoid open flames when melting wax. Use a double boiler.
- Ensure appropriate ventilation for this activity.

Water-Based Paints

- Use formaldehyde-free products, when possible.
- Some water-based paints may contain formaldehyde as a preservative, which may cause allergic reactions in sensitive individuals. If sensitive to this chemical, contact the manufacturer of the paints that you intend to use.
- Ensure appropriate ventilation for this activity.

Acrylics (Water-Based)

- Some contain small amounts of ammonia (as a stabilizer) and formaldehyde (as a preservative), which may cause respiratory irritation and may also cause allergies in sensitized individuals. If sensitive to these chemicals, contact the manufacturer of the paints that you intend to use.
- Ensure appropriate ventilation for this activity.
- Avoid using solvent-based acrylics, epoxy paints, oil paints that are not water-based, latex paints, and alkyds.

A Note on Papermaking

Papermaking

- Substances typically used in papermaking include alum (potassium aluminum sulfate), lye, ammonia, chlorine bleach, hydrogen peroxide, pigments, natural colorants/dyes, washing soda (sodium carbonate), acetic acid, and potassium ferricyanide.
- *Read the product label.* When possible, choose the safest materials available (e.g., those with few or no cautionary/warning labels).
- Household solutions of chlorine bleach (5%), ammonia (<3%), hydrogen peroxide (3%), and acetic acid (vinegar ~4–6%) may cause skin/eye, respiratory, and mucous membrane irritation. Concentrated solutions of these chemicals are corrosive.
- Washing soda and lye are corrosive.
- Some pigments may be hazardous. Use premixed pigments.
- Identify and avoid toxic woods and plants.
- Wear gloves, an apron, and goggles or a face shield, and have an eyewash and/or shower available.

- To avoid electrocution while working with electrical equipment, use electrical outlets protected by a ground fault circuit interrupter (GFCI).
- Noise and debris from beaters, macerators, and blenders may cause injury. Use proper machine guards and earplugs.

Marbling

- This involves floating paints on a layer of carrageenan gel on water. Typically, paint adhesion is improved by sponging the paper with alum (potassium aluminum sulfate).
- Some pigments and dyes may be toxic.
- *Read the product label.* When possible, choose the safest materials available (e.g., those with few or no cautionary/warning labels).
- Alum may cause skin irritation or allergic reactions.
- Mix powdered pigments in a glove box (a sealed transparent container with built-in gloves used to manipulate materials) or, when possible, use premixed paints.

Again, this is just a smattering of the information on arts and crafts materials that is available from the U.S. Government Publishing Office. More will be specified in later chapters on the materials. But when in doubt, research, research, research.

References

U.S. Consumer Product Safety Commission (CPSC). (n.d.). *Art and Craft Safety Guide.* Pub. No. 5015. Retrieved February 16, 2016 from www.cpsc.gov/PageFiles/112284/5015.pdf.

U.S. Government Publishing Office. (1988). Public Law 100-695. Retrieved February 16, 2016 from www.gpo.gov/fdsys/pkg/STATUTE-102/pdf/STATUTE-102-Pg4568.pdf.

U.S. Government Publishing Office. (2012). 15 USC 1277 – Labeling of art materials. Retrieved February 16, 2016 from www.gpo.gov/fdsys/granule/USCODE-2011-title15/USCODE-2011-title15-chap30-sec1277.

Websites

Spinal Cord Injury Zone, "Motorised Mouth Painting Easel: www.spinalcordinjuryzone.com/videos/11880/motorised-mouth-painting-easel (Retrieved February 16, 2016).

2 Developmental Stages, Assessment, and Holistic Considerations

> You cannot predict the outcome of human development. All you can do is, like a farmer, create the conditions under which it will begin to flourish.
>
> Ken Robinson, "Bring on the Learning Revolution!" TEDTalks (2010)

Chronosystem Patterning and Genograms

What you do changes you. Fundamentally, what you resolve to do, how you approach life, and what you come to value are of great consequence. In life, we are in relationship with *everything*: the dirt on the floor; the humidity in the air; the parched, dusty cornfields; the sweat trickling down our brow; the reverberation of a piano's key; even the words on the paper from which we read.

William James wrote, "The greatest discovery of my generation is that a human being can alter his life by altering his attitudes of mind" (1890). That quote was prophetic. In essence, James, the prominent nineteenth-century American psychologist, was talking about epigenetics, the study of heritable changes in the gene activity that are *not* caused by changes in the DNA sequence; in effect, these changes in gene expression (or cellular phenotype) evolve from other causes. Epigenetics renders our brains (and bodies) as flexible, capable of adapting, evolving and changing. Given how important mapping out the psychosocial background of our patients is in understanding their psychodynamics and life story, at intake, I create a three-generation genogram (using the software program Genogram Analytics). The reason is simple: we do not exist in isolation from one another. We are a product of not just our genetics but also our upbringing (McCartney et al., 1990). A genogram is a three-generation (minimum) visual map of an identified person's (IP) family system (Butler, 2008; Jolly et al., 1980):

> A genogram (also known as a McGoldrick–Gerson study, a Lapidus schematic or a family diagram) is a pictorial display of a person's family relationships and medical history. It goes beyond a traditional family tree by allowing the user to visualize hereditary patterns and psychological factors

> that punctuate relationships. It can be used to identify repetitive patterns of behavior and to recognize hereditary tendencies.
>
> (Wikipedia, n.d.)

Moreover, this construct can include psychological scores (intelligence quotient scores such as an WISC-R), strengths and weaknesses, *DSM-5* information from an attending psychiatrist, and visual symbols that help track conflicts handed down from generation to generation. (Therapists who function from a family systems platform routinely use genograms.) In addition, a chronological timeline can be created which maps out any nodal events that have influenced the patient's history. So, whenever possible, I invite the nuclear family system to participate in therapy.

According to Sluzki (1983), family therapy represents an entirely new paradigm in conceptualizing human problems, understanding behavior and developments, and a patient's symptoms and resolution. Looking at a family from these perspectives allows for a wholly different method of collecting and interpreting information and data. The family as a functioning (or dysfunctional) transactional system and entity in and of itself, more than the sum of its individual components, provides the context for individual functioning (or lack thereof) and often, development (arrested or age appropriate).

While often someone is considered the IP, if one views this individual in relation to his/her family system, then the person is seen in a much fuller context. Since we do not operate in isolation from others and are a product of genetics,

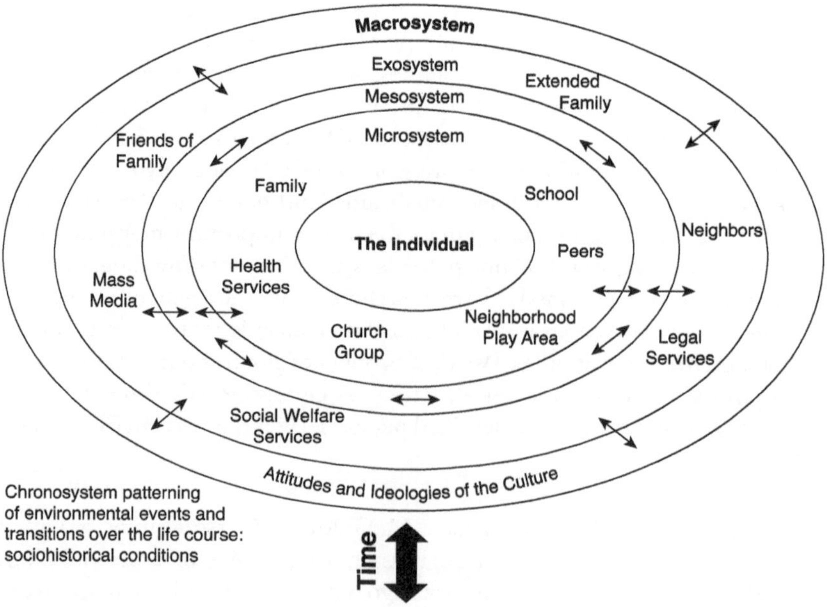

Figure 2.1 The chronosystem patterning of the individual.

psychosocial systems, culture, belief systems and our environs, to view someone in isolation from these different systems is indeed a mistake. Figure 2.1 is a map of how to view someone in relation to the chronosystem patterning that impacts our functioning. (A chronosystem links individual and families by social interdependence, sociohistorical influences, environmental events and transitions over the life course.) Figure 2.1 is based on Bronfenbrenner's ecological theory of development (Bronfenbrenner, 1994).

Using a genogram as a construct, a clinician can also include psychological scores (intelligence quotient scores), strengths and weaknesses, *DSM-5* information from the attending psychiatrist, and visual symbols that help you track conflicts handed down from generation to generation (McGoldrick et al., 2008). As well, a chronological timeline can be created which maps out any nodal events that have affected the patient's history. These days, the instructions are so simple that the most basic steps can even be found on the internet. While simple instructions may be offered, after combing through different programs, I have settled on using the Genogram Analytics software program (www.genogramanalytics.com) created by Loie West, Ph.D., psychologist, and her software/engineer husband, Tom West. The reasons are ease of use, including tutorials on YouTube, and the software's ability to be understood by educationalists and professionals alike. This software program easily allows for pertinent information to be added to the visual map. Should more information be necessary to complete an IP's timeline, a separate addendum can be created. The Genogram Analytics software package automatically creates a key in the document for occupation, education, cause of death, disease, psychiatric conditions, etc. As can be seen from the example genogram (Figure 2.2), pertinent information is available for the practitioner to use and the program automatically employs keys and is color-coded for descriptive understanding.

Assessments as Indices to Understanding Your Patient(s)

While more complete information on the use of genograms and assessment can be forward in *The Art Therapists' Primer: A Clinical Guide to Writing Assessments, Diagnosis, and Treatment* (Horovitz, 2014), I am offering (herein) the bare bones of what a therapist needs to construct a baseline of where to start (both developmentally and with art materials). But I would highly recommend that the reader also read the aforementioned book since it is filled with information on numerous assessments, both quantitative and qualitative, that can be used to ascertain information on your patient.

In 1987, I discussed the importance of assessment in the *Journal of Art Therapy* (Horovitz-Darby, 1987) and in 1988, I published the first edition of the CATA (Cognitive Art Therapy Assessment), which has since been refined in my 2014 publication. While the CATA is more of a qualitative instrument, it is guised as a studio activity and therefore is less anxiety-provoking than standardized tests that enforce (for example) drawing a person picking an apple from a tree (PPAT) (Gantt & Tabone, 1998).

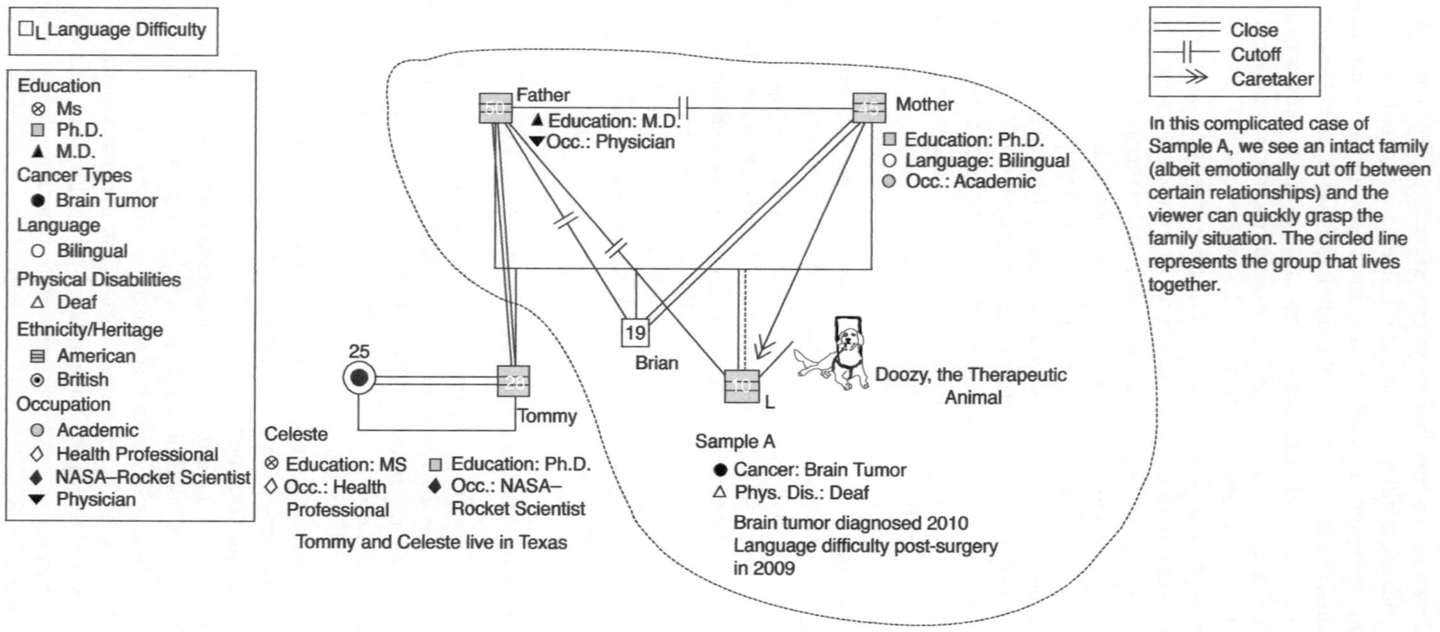

Figure 2.2 An example genogram.

Essentially, the CATA can provide a clinician with the following information to consider when deciding what art materials might best assist the patient:

1 Outstanding developmental capacities, deficits, deviations, visual-motor functioning. Developmental stage as seen in artwork. If deficits are indicated, is it possible that they are constitutional and/or emotional, cultural?
2 Self-image: sexual identity, self-esteem, ego ideals.
3 Perception of self in relation to others. Individuation, strong emotional attachments, symbiosis?
4 Sense of reality. Distortions of self and body parts, depersonalization?
5 Thought processes, ability to conceptualize, memory, judgment, concrete or abstract thinking?
6 Defenses – and dangers defended against.
7 Capacity for other gratifications – not art but playful manipulation of materials.
8 Potential to learn, to master, to function on a higher level, environmental, or cultural factors that might be influential.
9 Temperamental assessment as seen in art session, mood quality – exuberant, hesitant, overwhelmed by anxiety, etc. Activity level – hyperactive, deliberate, reflective, attention span approach or withdrawal? Adaptability or construction?
10 Capacity for ego gratification through art. Capacity for ego maturation through art.

While the standardized instrument, the PPAT, can be tied to specific graphic equivalents of symptoms from the *DSM-5* and in fact has proven useful in diagnosing the art even when an art therapist is not present (Gussak, 2013), patients are often "put off" by standardized tests and thus respond better to assessments that are more studio-based in measure (such as the previously mentioned CATA). Being able to tie this artwork (at least the two-dimensional work yielded from the CATA) to the PPAT is especially affirming and generally yields the same results when comparing it to Lowenfeld and Brittain's developmental scales (Lowenfeld & Brittain, 1975), Horovitz's scales (Horovitz, 2014), or other measures that are available. See Table 2.1 for more information on comparative developmental measures that also include moral and spiritual dimensions.

Both Gantt (2001) and Horovitz (2014) have published on the validity of tying the PPAT to subjective measures. I synthesized that in Horovitz (2014), tying the PPAT's formal element scale measures to the HTP (House–Tree–Person) test, the KFD (Kinetic Family Drawing), the ATDA (Art Therapy Dream Assessment), the BATA (Belief Art Therapy Assessment), the CATA (Cognitive Art Therapy Assessment), and the Hanes Road Test. In essence, it can be tied to any subjective instrument noting the features I indicate in Table 2.2.

In sum, art therapy assessments can range from art-based clinical interviews (Betts, 2003; Deaver & Bernier, 2014; Hinz, 2009; Horovitz-Darby, 1987, 1988; Horovitz, 2004, 2014) to observational interviews (Kramer & Schehr,

Table 2.1 Comparative stages of development.

Eras/Ages	*Erikson*	*Piaget*	*Kohlberg*	*Lowenfeld & Brittain*	*Fowler*	*Gantt & Tabone*	*Horovitz*
Infancy (0–1.5 yrs)	Basic Trust vs. Basic Mistrust (Hope)	Sensorimotor Stage		Scribble Stage: Beginning of Self-Expression (0–2 yrs)	Stage 0: Primal or Undifferentiated (0–2 yrs)	Rating 0: Cannot Be Rated	
Early Childhood (2–6 yrs)	Autonomy vs. Shame & Doubt Initiative vs. Guilt (Purpose)	Preoperational or Intuitive	*Preconventional Level* 1. Heteronomous Morality	Preschematic Stage: First Representations (4–7 yrs)	Stage 1: Intuitive-Projective (3–7 yrs)	Rating 1: Scribbles/Masses Stage Rating 2: Geometric Shapes (4–6 yrs)	
Childhood (7–12 yrs)	Industry vs. Inferiority	Concrete Operational	2. Instrumental Exchange *Conventional Level* 3. Mutual Interpersonal Relationships	The Schematic Stage: Formed Concepts (7–9 yrs)	Stage 2: Mythic-Literal (mostly in school children)	Rating 3: Latency Age/Logical and Proportionate	
Adolescence (13–21 yrs)	Identity vs. Role Confusion (Fidelity)	Formal Operational	4. Social System and Conscience	The Gang Age: Dawning Realism (9–12 yrs)	Stage 3: Synthetic-Conventional (12–adulthood)	Rating 4: Adolescence/ Realism	
Young Adulthood (21–35 yrs)	Intimacy vs. Isolation (Love)		*Post-Conventional Principled Level* 5. Social Contract, Individual Rights	Pseudo-Naturalistic Stage: Age of Reasoning (12–14 yrs)	Stage 4: Individuative-Reflective (mid 20s–late 30s)		

Adulthood (35–60 yrs)	Generativity vs. Stagnation (Care)			Adolescent Art: Period of Decision (14–17 yrs)	Stage 5: Conjunctive (mid-life crisis)		
Maturity (60+ yrs)	Integrity vs. Despair (Wisdom)		Universal Ethical Principles				Adult Stage: Formation in the World (8–adulthood)
					Stage 6: Universalizing Enlightenment	Rating 5: Adult/ Some Artistic Sophistication	Artistic Stage: Formed Art, Any Age (generally in adolescence through adulthood)

N.B.: Regarding the Stages of Development as outlined by Lowenfeld and Brittain: While they do not describe this as a stage, the *Brain-Injured Stage* can occur at any age; Horovitz has described this in her lectures as consisting of organic qualities, where objects float on the page (e.g., a lack of order and an ungrounded quality to the artwork is pervasive in the representations, be they two- or three-dimensional.) As well, since they do not hallmark the *Adult or Artistic Stages of Development*, Horovitz does, since she feels that these stages vary dramatically from the Adolescent period, the last stage, which they described.

1983; Rubin, 1984). Such approaches to assessment typically involve offering patients a variety of directives using both two- and three-dimensional media. Extrapolations about patient functioning are distilled via the art therapist's analysis of the presented artwork, observations of patient comportment and approach to the art media, the art therapist's knowledge of the projective media literature, and the art therapist's evaluation of the patient–therapist interaction. In discussing this, Deaver (2016) raises this very important question: "Is it ethical to make decisions about patient care based upon assessments that do not have sufficiently sound psychometric properties? Are we placing our patients and even our profession at risk by doing so?" (p. 740). Furthermore, Deaver suggests that cross-cultural considerations need to be considered, something that I raised with Linda Gantt (at the 2013 American Art Therapy Association Conference regarding the PPAT), and I subsequently added (with her blessing) multicultural

Table 2.2 The Horovitz Adapted Formal Elements Chart for Non-Standardized Assessments.

Formal Element Scale	*HTP*	*KFD*	*ATDA*	*BATA*	*CATA*	*Road*
Prominence of Color	✓ chromatic	✓ chromatic**	✓	✓	✓ chromatic**	✓
Color Fit	✓ chromatic	✓ chromatic**	*	*	*	✓
Implied Energy	✓	✓	✓	✓	✓	✓
Space	✓	✓	✓	✓	✓	✓
Integration	✓	✓	*	*	*	✓
Logic	✓	✓	*	*	*	✓
Realism	✓	✓	*	*	*	*
Problem-Solving	✓	✓	*	*	*	*
Developmental Level	✓	✓	✓	✓	✓	✓
Details of Objects and Environment	✓	✓	*	*	*	✓
Line Quality	✓	✓	✓	✓	✓	✓
Person	✓	✓	*	*	*	*
Rotation	✓	✓	*	*	*	*
Perseveration	✓	✓	✓	✓	✓	✓

* This scale may or may not apply based on the patient's response (e.g., abstraction, etc.).

** While the KFD and the CATA (drawing subtest) are achromatic assessments, often art therapists allow for color usage in this battery.

N.B.: Donna Betts has adapted her own version of the FEATS for use with the Face Stimulus Assessment (FSA), which is discussed in Chapter 14 of Horovitz, 2014.

markers to the PPAT since there were insufficient skin colors available in the prescribed (Mr. Sketch™) markers for the battery (Horovitz, 2014). And while Deaver (2016) suggests creating an international repository (the International Art Therapy Research Database (IATRD, www.arttherapyresearch.com)) for housing normative art therapy assessment samples, the repository faces an enormous hurdle complicated by HIPAA laws and regulations governing institutional review boards in the US. Yet, the idea of sharing such wealth with other practitioners could yield more and improved psychometric measures that would indeed advance the field of art therapy.

Development

Somatic Issues, Belief Systems, and Holistic Considerations

Doris Arrington (2016) sums up development by stating, "from infants to seniors, humans age at different rates, and therefore chronological age is an imperfect indicator of functional age" (p. 296). In that chapter, Arrington concisely describes the developmental markers in art ranging from preschool to Thanatos. But for condensing and synthesizing developmental art levels, *nothing* beats Lowenfeld and Brittain's art education source (1975). Still, Klorer (2000) takes artistic development a step further. While not calling it mirror neurons, she states, "I know what it feels like to make cathartic, angry pictures . . . so when a patient does so, I experience kinesthetic empathy" (p. x). She continues, "When art-making goes beyond throwing of clay and smearing of paint and is redirected and channeled into an art piece . . . that is where the healing takes place" (p. 6). This is what Edith Kramer (1975) referred to as sublimation versus formed expression.

Klorer, no stranger to somatic issues that arise in art therapy (which often include trauma), uses a Co-OperBlanket® in order to allow a child an opportunity to explore, expand touch and interaction with others, and "experiment with closeness and distance" (2000, p. 65). The Co-OperBlanket® can be used successfully between therapist and patient no matter what the latter's age. Since I am also a trained yoga therapist, I have used these bands in yoga therapy and also when I combine these with art therapy sessions (Horovitz & Elgelid, 2015). I have individual bands ranging from size small to large, a two-person Co-OperBlanket® for couples or therapist–patient interaction, and a large Co-OperBlanket® that can house 15 people for groups.

Using the Co-OperBlanket® invites opportunities for exploring physicality and somatic and traumatic issues, and its impact on development and movement provides the therapist with yet more indices for exploring the whole person. Our bodies inform the gut, long considered the second brain (Gershon, 1999) and as a creative art therapist and trained yoga therapist, I involve the entire person: mind, body, and spirit.

The reasons for this are myriad but in my first book, *Spiritual Art Therapy: An Alternate Path* (Horovitz, 2004), I laid the groundwork for examining the whole person via the Belief Art Therapy Assessment (BATA). The BATA explores

Figure 2.3 The author and patients using a Co-OperBlanket® in therapy.

issues of spirituality, religiosity, and/or belief systems when they move to the forefront of patient issues.

Indeed, in the past, religious and spiritual needs were entrusted to the clergy. Baptism, last rites, confirmation, communion, and even prayer are often delegated to religious leaders. This has created a fissure for any clinician who has faced a patient's spiritual questions, struggle with faith, and/or desire for forgiveness. There have been several options:

1 Ignore the spiritual dimension of the patient.
2 Chalk up the patient's thinking as floridly psychotic.
3 Refer the patient to a clergy person without participating in that aspect of care (thus defeating a systemic approach).
4 Collaborate with a clergy person and work out an interdisciplinary approach to treatment.
5 Attempt to spiritually counsel the patient.

Often, I choose number 5. Thus, I am making the assumption that spiritual care is a legitimate part of health care. Even though the clergy has a specified role in this arena, I propose that the spiritual needs of a patient require attention and treatment by the entire health care team. (Indeed, I have also invoked the clergy to help: years ago, while treating a family that was contending with mourning issues related to the death of their unborn infant, I invited the family's priest to attend the graveside visit so that the funeral process could be recreated and cast in a different light.) From a systemic perspective, an interdisciplinary and communal approach to treating an IP within a family systems framework is essential to the treatment of the whole person. Moreover, in order to accomplish such a formidable task, incorporating the spiritual, belief, and religious components into treatment requires a tool for assessing whatever nodal events contributed to the disorder and disease of the person. While the BATA offers an instrument for estimation, the reader may not be comfortable with continued exploration of a patient's spiritual belief system. If, in fact, this is the case, *then* one needs to embrace an interdisciplinary approach and rely on the skills and talents of other professionals within the community. *(N.B.: It is important to note that I conduct the BATA only when the patient questions or brings up his/her belief/spiritual dimension in interview or within the aforementioned testing component. Moreover, it is conducted only when the information might lead to an improved understanding of the patient as opposed to contributing to further deterioration of his/her condition.)* Even after the patient reveals his/her spiritual struggle by way of the BATA, it is wholly possible that he/she may not be ready to explore the "spiritual dimension" since this involves abstract thinking. If, in fact, the patient's thinking is formal, rigid, and concrete, then the therapist needs to walk this line with trepidation and *always* respect the patient's lead.

Mourning and Loss

Analyzing a patient and his/her family system via its communication style is crucial to family art therapy with any population. For example, modes of communication employed by family members may vary and the range of language systems may be expansive, circumscribed, bimodal, or virtually absent (Horovitz-Darby, 1991). This finding cannot be underestimated. Separate communication modes contribute to alienation, isolation, and linear punctuation. Thus, operating within an individual versus a communal construct can exacerbate and contribute to such a divisive position. Instead, transcending toward community, be it secular or religious, might help restore holistic functioning.

In order to create such "circular reciprocity" (Arrington, 1991) and envelop heteromorphic thinking, one needs to shake up the system – reframe it, if you will. Yet, any attempt to recast the family communication system threatens the homeostasis and established "balance of power" among family members (Harvey, 1984).

Investigating that distribution of power, which sustains the family myth of the IP as the root cause, aids the clinician in recasting the IP as no longer "sick." Moreover, while analyzing this situation, the therapist generally runs into mourning and loss issues that were somehow never resolved. Although the origins of these issues always vary, deep in the chronological timeline of the family, they can always be found. And, so before a patient or system can be edged toward recovery, inspection and examination is required to repair the damage. Like the mechanic attempting to decipher the misfiring of an engine, the therapist must begin to unseat these fittings and reassemble the engine parts with doses of empathy and emotional resonance.

Beginning with loss reconnects the patient to his/her very origin of dis-ease (e.g., symptomatic discomfort) and sets the stage for inclusion of the spiritual dimension. If one skips over these elements too quickly, then the work is not only hampered but spiritual evolution is impeded. As Moore (1992) suggests, the work of therapists would change radically "if we thought about it as ongoing care rather than as a quest for a cure" (p. 19).

Whether or not the therapist chooses to employ spiritual and holistic work from the perspective of conducting the BATA or involving the spiritual dimension is a matter determined by the patient and the clinician; but clearly, the therapist needs to move through this stratum mindful of the patient's apprehensions and defenses. Indeed, it becomes an approach–avoidance dance where often the patient and supportive therapist take two steps forward and two steps backward. While mourning may take on a restorative quality, leveling the pain attached to the loss (whatever form it takes: divorce, death, sexual trauma, or the like) is tantamount to crushing the issues and symptoms attached to that bereavement. But I contend that a focus on mourning and loss issues cannot be ignored and *has* to be the principal step in recovery. Without this primacy, there may be change, but *not* resolution. Instead, the symptoms will manifest repeatedly until the feelings connected to these losses are aired, examined, and most importantly *accepted*. It is then *and only then* that the real work of therapy can begin.

More information on developmental standards and these aforementioned issues will be explored as we move into Chapter 3. Additionally, those norms will be tied to case studies and my methodologies that have evolved in the 40 years of my career as an art therapist.

References

Arrington, D. (1991). Thinking systems – seeing systems: An integrative model for systemically oriented art therapy. *The Arts in Psychotherapy, an International Journal, 18*(3), 201–211.

Arrington, D. (2016). The developmental journey. In D. E. Gussak & M. L. Rosal (Eds.), *The Wiley handbook of art therapy* (pp. 201–209). Malden, MA: John Wiley & Sons, Ltd.

Betts, D. (2003). Developing a projective drawing test: Experiences with the Face Stimulus Assessment (FSA). *Art Therapy: Journal of the American Art Therapy Association, 20*(2), 77–82.

Bronfenbrenner, U. (1994). Ecological models of human development. In *The International encyclopedia of education* (pp. 37–43), Vol. 3, 2nd Ed. Oxford: Elsevier.

Butler, J. (2008). The family diagram and genogram: Comparisons and contrasts. *American Journal of Family Therapy, 36*(3), 169–180.

Deaver, S. (2016). The need for norms in formal art therapy assessment. In D. E. Gussak

& M. L. Rosal (Eds.), *The Wiley handbook of art therapy* (pp. 600–606). Malden, MA: John Wiley & Sons, Ltd.

Deaver, S., & Bernier, M. (2014). The art therapy–projective imagery assessment. In L. Handler & A. Thomas (Eds.), *Drawings in assessment and psychotherapy: Research and application* (pp. 131–147). New York, NY: Routledge.

Gantt, L. M. (2001). The Formal Elements Art Therapy Scale: A measurement system for global variations in art. *Art Therapy: Journal of the American Art Therapy Association, 18*(1), 50–55.

Gantt, L., & Tabone, C. (1998). *The Formal Elements Art Therapy Scale: The rating manual.* Morgantown, WV: Gargoyle Press.

Gershon, M. (1999). *The second brain: A groundbreaking new understanding of nervous disorders of the stomach and intestine.* New York, NY: Harper Perennial.

Gussak, D. (2013). *Art on trial: Art therapy in capital murder cases.* New York, NY: Columbia Press.

Harvey, M. A. (1984). Family therapy with deaf persons: The utilization of an interpreter. *Family Process, 23*(June) 205–221.

Hinz, L. D. (2009). *The expressive therapies continuum: A framework for using art in therapy.* New York, NY: Routledge.

Horovitz-Darby, E. G. (1987). Diagnosis and assessment: Impact on art therapy. *Journal of Art Therapy,* October, 127–137.

Horovitz-Darby, E. G. (1988). Art therapy assessment of a minimally language-skilled deaf child. In *Proceedings from the 1988 University of California's Center on Deafness Conference: Mental Health Assessment of Deaf Clients: Special Conditions* (pp. 72–99). Little Rock, AR: ADARA.

Horovitz-Darby, E. G. (1991). Family art therapy within a Deaf system. *Arts in Psychotherapy, 18,* 251–261.

Horovitz, E. G. (2004). *Spiritual art therapy: An alternate path.* Springfield, IL: Charles C. Thomas.

Horovitz, E. G. (Ed.). (2014). *The art therapists' primer: A clinical guide to writing assessments, diagnosis, and treatment* (2nd Ed.). Springfield, IL: Charles C. Thomas.

Horovitz, E. G., & Elgelid, S. (Eds.). (2015). *Yoga therapy: Theory and practice.* New York, NY: Routledge.

James, W. (1890). *Principles of psychology.* Digital version. Retrieved March 28, 2017 from http://psychclassics.yorku.ca/James/Principles/index.htm.

Jolly, W., Froom, J., & Rosen, M. G. (1980). The genogram. *Journal of Family Practice, 10*(2), 251–255.

Klorer, G. P. (2000). *Expressive therapy with troubled children.* New York, NY: Rowman & Littlefield.

Kramer, E. (1975). *Art as therapy with children.* New York, NY: Schocken Books.

Kramer, E., & Schehr, J. (1983). An art therapy evaluation session for children. *American Journal of Art Therapy, 23*(1), 3–12.

Lowenfeld, V., & Brittain, W. L. (1975). *Creative and mental growth* (6th Ed.). New York, NY: Macmillan.

McCartney, K., Harris, M., & Bernieri, F. (1990). Growing up and growing apart: A developmental meta-analysis of twin studies. *Psychological Bulletin, 107*(2), March, 226–237.

McGoldrick, M., Gerson, R., & Petry, S. (2008). *Genograms: Assessment and intervention* (3rd Ed.). New York, NY: W. W. Norton & Company.

Moore, T. (1992). *Care of the soul: A guide for cultivating depth and sacredness in everyday life.* New York, NY: HarperCollins.

Robinson, K. (2010, May). Bring on the learning revolution!. TEDTalks. Retrieved February 2, 2017 from www.youtube.com/watch?v=kFMZrEABdw4.

Rubin, J. (1984). *Child art therapy*. New York, NY: Van Nostrand Reinhold.

Sluzki, C. E. (1983). Process, structure and world views: Toward an integrated view of systemic models in family therapy. *Family Process*, *22*(4), 469–476.

Websites

Genogram Analytics: www.genogramanalytics.com (Retrieved March 28, 2017).

International Art Therapy Research Database (IATRD): www.arttherapyresearch.com (Retrieved March 28, 2017).

Wikipedia: http://en.wikipedia.org/wiki/Genogram (Retrieved July 9, 2017).

3 Basic Materials and Techniques

Strategies and Case Studies

> I use all sorts of things to work with: old brooms, old sweaters, and all kinds of peculiar tools and materials . . . I paint to excite myself, and make something for myself.
>
> attributed to Francis Bacon, quoted in Sam Piyasena and Beverly Philp, *Just Paint It!* (2014)

Introduction

Over the years, I have learned a lot from my readings and also many of my students. One of my students, now a respected colleague, Jennifer DeLucia, used to talk about the concept of "making special." I loved that term and still do. To explain it more fully, I offer a quote from Ellen Dissanyake:

> making important activities special has been basic and fundamental to human evolution and existence, and . . . while making special is not strictly speaking in all cases art, it is true that art is *always* an instance of making special. To understand art in the broadest sense, then, as a human proclivity, is to trace its origin to making special, and I will argue that making special was often inseparable from and intrinsically necessary to the control of the material conditions of subsistence that allowed humans to survive.
>
> (1992, p. 92)

Through image, a more common language than words, in that deep unconscious primal place, we human beings return to the differentiated state where we are working with essence to create healing; during the process of realizing the image and embodying it in the creation of art, we re-differentiate who we are as selves, coming up different, healed, more integrated, recreated. As the reader begins to turn his/her attention toward art materials and how they are utilized in the art therapy sessions, it is important to note that when "formed art" expression (Kramer, 1975) occurs, something else happens to the viewer. It is a secondary gain, which my dear, departed friend, Don Jones, and I used to call "aesthetic arrest." You may have experienced that feeling when (for example) you were awed by a sunset, or a painting moved you beyond verbal expression, or a musical piece left you breathless. Such formidable experiences inform your humanity and in turn make you special.

Where to Draw the Line, and the Basics of Setting Up Your Studio for Sessions

When a patient is in a state of dis-ease (Horovitz, 1999), it becomes all too easy to pathologize via the diagnosis as well as through the interpretation of the art:

- Unless we look for strengths in the medical and psychosocial histories, we can be trapped in the spiraling mentality of looking at a patient's symptoms and diagnostic classification instead of operating from the viewpoint of wellness.
- I caution the art therapist to beware of this trap, no matter whether an incipient student or a seasoned traveler. It is all too easy to fall victim to the danger of "fitting into" this methodology of treatment.

While it is important to understand a patient's dis-ease, it is often customary to be swayed by diagnostic indicators and definition both in terms of expected course of treatment and expected outcome, thus contributing to failure.

Setting Up the Studio: Important Considerations

Regardless of the above, one must consider diagnosis and possibly developmental arrest at the outset of treatment and the subsequent development (and/or regression) that can unfold when the patient waffles in recovery. These things are not easily taught. Over time, therapists come to understand this approach–avoidance dance. As well, there is something that seasoned therapists call "doorknob therapy." These are the crystalline moments that generally occur within the last five minutes of the session: a patient offers a pearl of insight into his/her problems or reveals a nodal issue or event and then heads out the door. Fortunately, if this occurs through the art, you have a permanent record of that moment and you can bring it into the next session for both continuity and to pick up where you left off. This cannot be understated. Just as important, make sure that you (1) date all artwork created in sessions, (2) write process notes *immediately following* sessions (so the information is fresh), and (3) maintain a portfolio of the artwork so that both you and the patient can review the progress from beginning to end of treatment. That brings us to setting up the space and the parameters around treatment issues.

Regarding the Issue of Time in Therapy

To lower defenses, Dean (2016a) often provides timed warnings with the patient in a method called "In through the Backdoor." It requires the patient to create six images using scribbles or other marking techniques and to mark the back of the paper used with the time limits (1 minute; 45 seconds; 30 seconds; 15 seconds; 2 minutes; 1 minute) (pp. 84–85).

Figure 3.1 A journal drawing brought to a session by a 78-year-old patient. (Printed with permission.)

While this exercise might allay anxiety (or in fact exacerbate it), I always give five- to ten-minute warnings before the session's end, depending on the patient. (This is especially important to do with very young children, who often do not want to stop the creative process. Also adding a statement such as, "I know that it is hard for you to stop, but I will see you again next week," or whenever the next scheduled session is slated, can allay anxiety and prevent meltdowns.) Offering some drawing paper and materials to take home and/or making a journal for patients to use between sessions can be enormously helpful and provide connection and continuity between sessions. (Figure 3.1 shows an example of what a 78-year-old patient sketched in the journal I made for him between our sessions. Gifting patients with journals has often illuminated and informed the discussion in subsequent sessions.)

It is imperative to try and end on time (and while there may be exceptions, it is often seen as counterproductive to extend the session past the allotted time.) There are exceptions to extending the session for the patient's benefit – especially if what arises in those last moments is emergent, critical, and would be beneficial to explore. However, taking such actions to a supervisor, whether you are a beginning or an advanced therapist, can rule out countertransference on your part; although, you should note that there are some who see extension of the therapeutic hour as seductive: case closed. I make decisions about extending session time on a case-by-case basis. As Rubin (1998) has stated, flexibility is key to being a competent therapist. But if you doubt your actions (if you extend the time with your patient), take it to your supervisor for discussion. To this day, I still meet with peers to exchange supervision. Fresh eyes are always a welcome perspective on particularly tough cases. I will talk more about that in Chapter 4 when I discuss telehealth and digital applications. Discussing these issues with other clinicians, even if they are inexperienced with telehealth applications, has been extremely helpful in my private practice.

Vacations

If you are planning a vacation, you need to forewarn your patients so that they are psychologically prepared for the missed time with you. (Using or making a calendar for small children or developmentally or neurologically challenged patients is also very useful to concretize the time between appointments.)

On Attire, Clean-Up, and Maintaining the Studio

Involving the patient in the therapeutic clean-up of the studio is also an important ritual in ownership of both the art and the mess created. Furthermore, it is vital that the therapist mirrors proper attire and dons a smock to protect his/her clothing so that the patient(s) will do the same. The fundamental thing is to always be early for your sessions; a half-hour is my bare minimum. This enables you to set up the space, re-read notes from previous sessions, and make sure that all art materials are in good working order. This might involve something as mundane as sharpening all colored pencils. No, I am not kidding: these little actions speak boatloads to the patient and metaphorically state that you care enough to offer the art materials in their best working order. (There is nothing worse than working with hardened clay when you want it to be pliable.)

So as a result, the art therapist needs to know all about the materials he/she is planning to use – not just their properties but also how to maintain them, etc. (Remember the old adage that you cannot take your patients any further than you have gone yourself.) So this might mean continuing education with a variety of materials. (In a pinch, YouTube videos come in very handy for on-the-spot review.) But ample preparation (e.g., practicing with the media) allows you to familiarize yourself with the properties and applications of the materials that you are using. (I cannot tell you how many of my students have arrived unprepared with the most basic knowledge of art materials, some never having worked with paint, clay, or even papier-mâché!) Learning how to operate and maintain equipment (machines, kilns, etc.) also falls under this domain. Your job description as an art therapist implies knowing the properties of the art materials that you are offering and keeping the safety of yourself and your patient paramount.

Establishing Rules and Etiquette for Groups

In some instances, depending on the nature of a group, rules need to be posted. Generally, I prefer to avoid this as it smacks of punitive associations and instead outline the rules of the group at the outset, reinforcing them verbally if needed over time. However for a rudimentary start, I offer a preliminary example below:

- Please respect the artwork of others and do not work on anyone else's artwork unless invited to participate. Please use all art materials appropriately (e.g., use tarps to protect surfaces, do not throw clay, etc.).

- Please wear a smock (or other equipment necessary – gloves, etc.) to protect yourself from unnecessary spills and mess.
- Listen respectfully to each person discuss his/her artwork.
- No aggression towards others or others' artwork will be tolerated.
- Be prepared to care for your materials, taking the time to clean up your materials and leave them in good working order for the next person or session.

Obviously, you can alter the rules to what suits the group that you are working with, but this should offer you a starting point.

Drawing: The Very Basics – Pencils, Erasers, Pastels, Charcoal, Markers, etc.

Considerations

Hinz (2016) stated, "In considering the needs and goals of the participant and the setting, the therapist needs to be able to select the appropriate media for a session" (p. 231). She also suggested that the therapist "lead by example" (p. 224). This is implicit when adopting what Edith Kramer would call the three-capped process. Kramer (1975) always talked about an art therapist being an artist, a teacher, and a therapist all at once. And this is exactly what Hinz (2016) referred to when suggesting use of media. She also recommended involving "breath awareness and biophysical feedback" to enhance skill building (p. 227). This has long been known as a Kramerian technique; in a video, *Edith Kramer: Art Tells the Truth* (LenFim Studio, 2011), you can witness how Kramer uses breath awareness and the body to warm up the patient for spontaneous art making. As her graduate student in 1977, I witnessed this firsthand; but viewing the "Mother of Art Therapy" in film should aid the reader's understanding of one way to involve breath awareness and inform biophysical feedback.

But first, you need to start with the person. How does the patient strike you? Does he/she seem to need structure? Here are some parameters to consider:

- Always start with dry materials when in doubt. Wet materials can stimulate regression. While this may be desirable in some situations, when you first meet a patient, it is always best to proceed with dry materials (pencil, crayons, markers, etc.) and then eventually lead up to more regressive materials (pastels, tempera paints, oil pastels, clay, papier-mâché, plaster, etc.).
- Color can lead to affect. (Even colored pencils can induce affect.)

Observe important details such as the following:

- motor dexterity and dependency needs;
- tenseness, impulsivity, and insecurities;
- change of tempo, spontaneity of behavior/comments, and detail of drawings.

It is also helpful to know the four stages of age progression in children, whether working with children or not:

1 pleasure from producing marks
2 imitative and reproductive drawings
3 learned phase (not always acquired)
4 graphic procedures based on design and balance.

(N.B.: Human Figure Drawings can also be analyzed for emotional indicators and cognitive information reflecting an individual's emotional conflicts and attitudes instead of merely a developmental milestone. See the work of Buck (1948), Machover (1949), Hammer (1980), and Horovitz (2014).)

Drawing Materials and the Bare Basics

Since drawing materials are so basic, I will cover the general considerations herein. Number 2 pencils used for mathematics and grammar school certainly can operate as drawing implements, but for true drafting I recommend having a variety of drawing materials available. *(N.B.: There are exceptions – for example, when conducting assessments such as the Bender-Gestalt II (Brannigan & Decker, 2003). Here one should use a Number 2 pencil as instructed in the battery.)*

Below are some items that the art therapist should consider having in his/her studio.

Pencils

- The following types of pencil should be available: a set of twelve pencils ranging from 6B, through 5B, 4B, 3B, 2B, B, HB, F, H, 2H, 4H, to 6H. The different hardness of the lead offers a variety of choices and results.
- Obviously, there are a variety of colored pencils available on the market but now there are even pencils that are loaded for watercolor and ink applications. These can work well when access to water is a hardship.

(N.B.: Derwent makes particularly good pencils for both watercolor and ink applications. Derwent's Inktense Pencils are terrific. They also make Graphitint Pencils, Onyx Pencils, Pastel Pencils, and very high-grade Studio Colored Pencils. While they are expensive, they are excellent quality and I would highly recommend them against the competition if you can afford them in your studio.)

Erasers

While Hymen Lipman of Philadelphia, Pennsylvania, patented the pencil-and-eraser on March 30, 1858 (today better known as the Number 2 pencil), it is highly recommended that art therapists provide erasers separate from their drawing pencils. Below are items that I would suggest having in your studio:

Figure 3.2 A 10-year-old boy's Kinetic Family Drawing, created using pencil: erasure, pressure, and subject matter suggest paranoia/hypervigilance around familial issues.

- charcoal, graphite, and pastel erasers (three different types for these media)
- dry cleaning eraser pads
- markerboard erasers
- pen and ink erasers
- pencil erasers (I prefer the General's Factis Extra Soft Eraser for least residue; there are also retractable and peel-off erasers).

Population Benefits and Contraindications

Drawing materials work well with almost any population. However, when working with an aggressive and/or possibly assaultive population, caution must be heeded even when working with the innocent pen or pencil. Pencils and pens can be used as weapons on others or for self-harm. Art therapists are advised to keep a vigilant eye on their patients at all times. I *never* turn my back on a patient even when getting art materials out. This calls for either knowing where your items are (if in a recessed shelf or closet) or having the patient(s) come up to the supply cabinet with you in order to keep a watchful eye on the patient(s) and the materials.

Crayons

As regards crayons, I recommend having the bare minimum: the eight-color set containing red, orange, yellow, blue, green, violet, brown, and black. *(N.B.: These are also the colors that should be offered when the chromatic HTP (House–Tree–Person) test is being conducted (Horovitz, 2014).)*

My personal favorites are the Crayola Jumbo size for their ease of use. Wax-based crayons have lots of options. For example, they can be used for melting in candle making or for batik when using them as a resist to water-based paints (poster or acrylic paints or even dyes). Figure 3.3 shows an example of this batik method created by a 7-year-old girl (white poster paint was painted over wax crayons to create a beautiful resist). This particular artwork was submitted for the Rhode Island Christmas stamp contest in 1975 and won! The child is shown proudly holding the artwork.

Figure 3.3 A batik resist example created with wax crayons and poster paint.

Step-by-Step Instructions for Crayon Batik

1. You will need: crayons, dark-colored water-soluble paint (and/or fabric dye), paper, a brush, and a damp cloth.
2. Draw and color an image, pressing hard on the crayons. You will want to fill the tooth of the paper with the wax.
3. Crumple up the paper and smooth it out.
4. Paint over with any dark water-soluble paint or dye, then wipe the paint away with a damp cloth.
5. When you wipe away the paint, it should settle wherever the wrinkles are, creating the batik textural look.
6. Consider the importance of color and value contrast; bold designs will work best.
7. The designs can vary from simple to complex, depending on the patient.

Population Benefits and Contraindications

A lot of art therapists avoid using crayons with older populations because it may make the person feel infantilized (memories of use are often from childhood). Instead, they may opt for oil-based crayons such as Cray-Pas, but these can be messy, which can be a drawback for some patients. Crayons can also be enormously freeing and yield self-expression and banter about the halcyon days, which could aid in both emotion and memory retrieval. Personally, I love crayons and many of my students also find great expression with this medium.

Below are some suggestions for types of crayon to have in your arsenal:

- water-soluble artist crayons
- wax-based artist crayons
- scholastic crayons
- fabric crayons
- Cray-Pas, oil-based crayons.

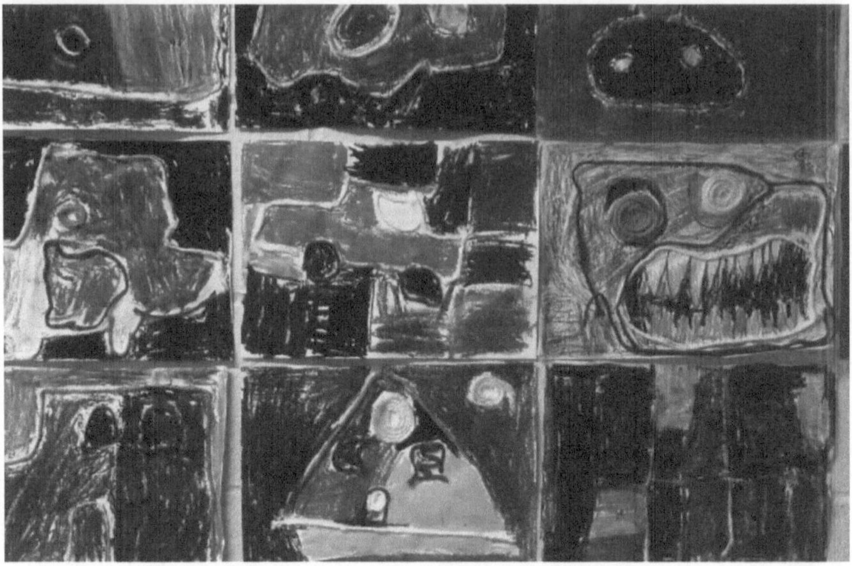

Figure 3.4 A beautiful example of artwork done by children (age 9) incorporating Cray-Pas as well as yarn to illuminate the design. (Printed with permission.)

Figure 3.5 A Deaf 17-year-old girl created this pastel and charcoal image of a rabbit, which led to her talking about how she felt when she fell down the rabbit hole of low self-esteem. (Printed with permission.)

Pastels and Charcoal

Again, there are a variety of pastels available on the market, from student-grade pastels to more professional sets such as Rembrandt Soft Pastels sets. Pastels are also available in pencil format, so, once again, mess (or lack of access to water) should be considered. Charcoal also comes in a variety of sizes and hardness (vine, willow, compressed, etc.) With both pastels and charcoal, the art therapist should have a tortillon available for blending either medium. (Paper towels work in a pinch if you don't have access to a tortillon.)

However, another consideration when working with these media is that they easily smudge and can only be made permanent with a fixative. Most art therapists do not have proper ventilation in their studios and so fixing a pastel or charcoal drawing requires going outside, lest the fumes waft. Often, to avoid fumes, I use a cheap pump hairspray to fix the image. However, it is still recommended that this be done with either proper ventilation and/or outside.

Population Benefits and Contraindications

Charcoal might be reserved for those who do not care about the regressive quality of the medium, and that can be any age. Artists or those with artistic leanings might be more comfortable with charcoal-based and pastel media. While both charcoal pencils and pastel pencils are available for those who need greater control, the therapist still might observe pushback from patients who struggle with control issues. On the other hand, to aid patients who are more reserved, charcoal and pastels might be just the ticket to allow for creative self-expression and creating a mess within a controlled and safe environment.

Markers

Markers have become incredibly sophisticated since Crayola offered a basic color set of 12. There are permanent markers, acrylic and oil paint markers (yes, markers filled with paint for those who prefer painting neatly without brushes), illustration and drafting markers, water-based markers, calligraphy markers, gel ink pen markers, etc. The list goes on and on. Markers have their uses, such as for the PPAT (Gannt & Tabone, 1998), and Crayola multicultural markers can be used to depict skin tones. However, I was mentored by the purist, Edith Kramer, who abhorred markers – and with good reason. Mixing the pigments is difficult at best since markers often do not blend and therefore can frustrate the patient and result in muddy quality. However, many art therapists prefer them because of their ease of use, non-messy qualities, and portability. (I recommend

Figure 3.6 An image created by a Deaf 14-year-old girl, illustrating her relationship with her father (on the right). Her sister (on the left), in the striped shirt and with a wider mouth, is placed at a distance, indicating the patient's desire to distance her sister from herself and her father. Note the conjoined ear between the patient and her father. (Printed with permission.)

having fine-point, medium-point, and broad-point markers on hand for those who cannot tolerate any sort of regression with messier dry materials.) But I prefer to avoid markers altogether when paints or color-loaded pencils (such as Derwent's) are readily available. (There are some instances when specific kinds of markers can be handy and I will get into these when I discuss Pébéo paint markers for fabric, porcelain, and glass creation. More on that in Chapter 4.)

Population Benefits and Contraindications

Markers are relatively transportable and easy to use. They range from water-soluble to permanent and oil-based. For these reasons, the art therapist should be aware of the limitations and uses of both types of marker. While they are relatively easy to use and less messy than traditional paints, they cannot truly be mixed without becoming muddy. Children, pre-pubescents, and adolescents particularly like working with this medium, and adults who are non-responsive to paints (watercolor, tempera, acrylic, or oil, etc.) respond well to markers. Some markers can be diluted with water for a more painterly effect.

Papier-Mâché

While papier-mâché may be considered a material used only in elementary schools, it is by far one of my favorite materials. There are many reasons for this, but they include cost (it is exceptionally cheap to make the paste), the abundance of paper materials (newspaper), and its availability. For starters, it is very accessible and the papier-mâché paste can be made from kitchen materials (flour and water – but a warning will follow about that), watered-down Elmer's Glue or a similar substance, and my personal favorite, Roman's GH-57 Universal wallpaper paste, which comes premixed in gallon containers. The latter also has a shelf life that exceeds that of flour and water or diluted Elmer's Glue. A warning to the reader: years ago, while vacationing with my siblings in our Adirondack property, I left my papier-mâché bowl outside to dry in the heat of the day. (The paste was made of flour and water.) But a critter, attracted to the flour, devoured half my day's work before I discovered the theft! Below are some of my favorite recipes for making papier-mâché pulp (a clay-like substance) superior to the commercially available pulp that is mixed with water. *(N.B.: When mixed with water, the premixed commercially available pulp produces dust and vapors, and is not patient-friendly. Instead, my papier-mâché pulp recipe is made from readily available materials, by recycling cardboard egg cartons or packaging materials and simply adding a bit of detergent and water until softened. See Figure 3.7, my recipe below, and Figure 3.8, showing my papier-mâché example.)*

Figure 3.7 Papier-mâché pulp mixture after soaking overnight.

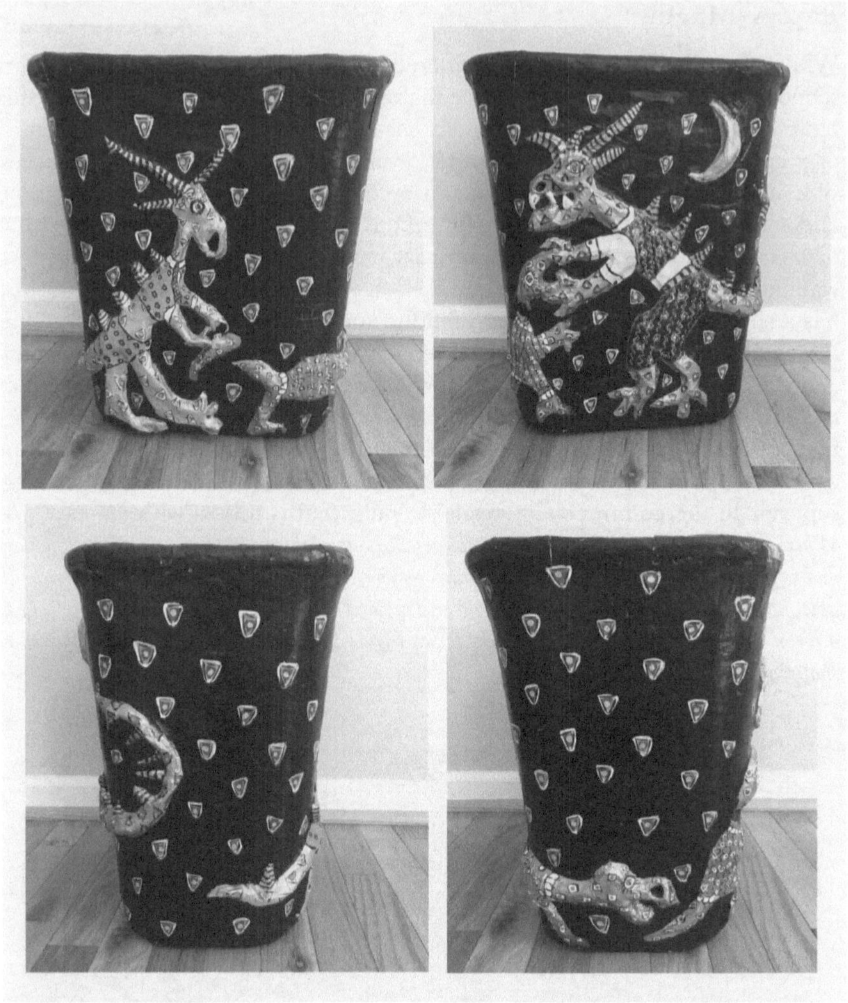

Figure 3.8 My example of a papier-mâché garbage can. Note how the papier-mâché pulp goes around the can from front and back to the can's sides (top, left to right).

Horovitz's Papier-Mâché Pulp Recipe

1 Take paper-based egg cartons and tear them up into small bits (you can easily do this while watching a movie!). Place in a large plastic baggie that has good closure.
2 Add about a quarter-cup of any kind of detergent. Add a bit more than a quarter-cup of water so that all of the egg-carton material is covered and soaked.

3 Leave for eight hours or overnight, and then pour out any excess detergent/water mixture. You are ready to use your papier-mâché pulp. It can be squeezed and formed into any shape and added to the body of the papier-mâché object covered with newspaper/glue binder.

(N.B.: My homemade papier-mâché pulp can be stored indefinitely and rewet when ready to use. I also often add newspaper over the papier-mâché pulp sculpting and tie it into the paper-mâché material underneath. This makes for a very smooth transition and takes on the professional look that one gets when sculpting with clay.)

Case Study Using Papier-Mâché

In this case, an 11-year-old boy in residential treatment struggled to accept his new status, a "ward of the state." So for many sessions, J disputed his state of literally being "homeless" and without family. As a result, creating home environments were extremely important to him. As shown in Figures 3.9 and 3.10, J created a horse made out of cardboard tubes, newspaper, and papier-mâché. After painting the horse, he decided next to tame this obvious stand-in for himself. He created a felt bridle and saddle. But still this was not enough. He decided that the horse needed a barn (i.e., home protection). I scoured the streets to find a large box suitable for the barn (home), and together

Figure 3.9 J's papier-mâché horse and symbolic stand-in for himself. (Printed with permission.)

Figure 3.10 J's papier-mâché horse gets a home. (Printed with permission.)

we fashioned and painted the house, filling the stall with mounds of cotton. In this instance, the papier-mâché barn was a project that took weeks from start to finish and offered J a sense of place, while simultaneously bolstering his self-esteem and creating fertile ground for him to discuss these very painful feelings of both rejection and longing.

Collage

In 1981, Helen Landgarten published a landmark book, *Clinical Art Therapy: A Comprehensive Guide*, and later (in 1993) published the Magazine Photo Collage (MPC) method in *Magazine Photo Collage: A Multicultural Assessment and Treatment Technique*. The MPC projective assessment had the therapist precut and sort through images from magazines and divide them into two labeled boxes (one for images of people and the other for images of miscellaneous items). Careful attention was paid to the selection of diversity in the images of people for gender, culture, facial expression and body placement, varied ages, etc. Furthermore, if the therapist wanted to flush out a specific agenda (e.g., substance abuse, eating disorders, divorce issues, etc.), then those images could be "planted" in the box (1993; pp. 6–11). The protocol had four tasks for the patient:

1 Choose images from the miscellaneous box, adhere them to the paper, and tell the therapist what comes to mind.
2 Choose a half-dozen or so images from the people box, adhere them to the paper, and comment on what the people are thinking or saying.

3 Choose another half-dozen images from the miscellaneous box, label them either "good" or "bad," and discuss the meaning of those images.
4 Select an image of a person and adhere it to the paper while telling the therapist what is happening to that person, how the situation will now change, and what will make it change.

Stallings modified Landgarten's process in 2009 in her work with dementia patients. Recently, she also wrote a poignant chapter on the use of collage and pointed out its adaptability as a "medium that works well with a variety of client populations and settings . . . [is] less threatening as a starting point [and could possibly] include the use of digital collages" (2016, pp. 252–253). I have also published extensively about the use of digital phototherapeutic/collage techniques in both art making and with patients (Horovitz, 2011, 2014, 2016.) In the lovely example shown in Figure 3.11, art therapist Donna Betts illustrates using a magazine for self-image photo collage where she directed another art therapist (Matthew Bernier) to capture her image. This method of using collage is a phototherapy technique where the maker (in this case, Donna) photo-directs the photographer (in this case, Matthew) how she wants to be digitally photographed.

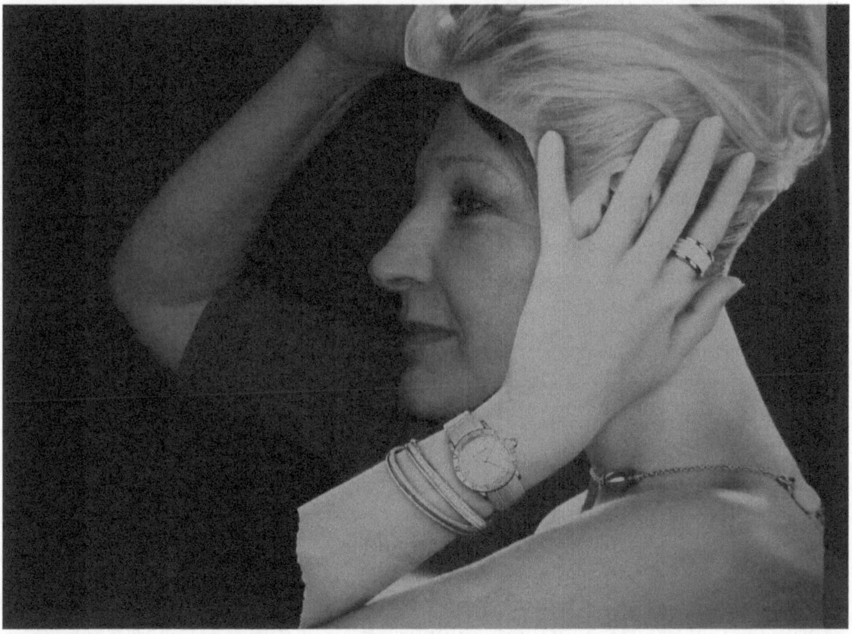

Figure 3.11 Donna Betts using phototherapy direction to create an image of herself, using magazine collage images. (Printed with permission.)

Figure 3.12 Digital artwork by Lani Gerrity Glanville. (Printed with permission.)

Population Benefits and Contraindications

Magazines and photo collage (think for example selfies, Instagram, and other apps available on the internet) can be utilized with almost any population imaginable. Magazines and images are accessible everywhere, including via computers and digital manipulations. It doesn't take a skilled art therapist to use magazine and/or photo collage techniques. On the contrary, collage/photo manipulation can be used by any therapist, and no training is necessary to utilize magazines for collage and/or assessment with patients. However, if one looks at the beautiful artwork of some digital collage manipulators, such as Lani Gerrity Glanville (see her blog at: http://14secretsforahappyartistslife.blogspot.com/), one can truly appreciate the artistic possibilities with this medium. Personally, I avoid using magazine collage materials as stipulated in the MPC method (Landgarten,1993); instead, I employ digital imagery and prefer the methodology used by Gerrity Glanville and similar art therapists to foster creativity and recovery in patients. (More will be covered regarding how to use digital applications in Chapter 4.)

Alcohol Inks

You can use alcohol inks for a variety of things, from decorating your own paper (think journal pages) to using on watercolor paper, specialty papers such as YUPO Synthetic, glass, polymer clay, and even ceramic tile. The commercial alcohol inks (such as Adirondack Ranger inks, which are quite superior) are rather expensive, but you can make them yourself. Below are some recipes. There are many different dilutions that you can do with the alcohol and ink. First and foremost, *before mixing* you should be wearing clothes that you don't mind staining, or a smock, as well as rubber or latex-free gloves.

DIY Alcohol Ink Recipes

You will need a 2 oz travel spray bottle from the dollar store (either the spray-pump kind or those that can pour the ink out) and 99% rubbing alcohol.

Alcohol Inks Using a Pen

1 Pull out the ink from a regular pen with pliers, cut it into pieces, and place them in the bottle.
2 Pour in 99% alcohol almost to the top.
3 Shake the mixture: the more it sits, the more ink concentrate you get!

Alcohol Inks Using a Pastel Stick

1 Fill the bottle three-quarters full with rubbing alcohol.
2 Break a pastel stick in half and place the pieces in the bottle.
3 Bubbles will emerge as the pastel disintegrates. Close it up and let it soak.
4 Shake the mixture: the more it sits, the more ink concentrate you get!

Alcohol Inks Using a Permanent Marker

1 Use a Sharpie permanent marker or a similar version from your local dollar store.
2 Using pliers, pull out the felt tip of the marker. If already saturated, then place this into the empty bottle.
3 Pull the marker apart. Snip the cotton tube that is inside into pieces and add to your bottle. Add alcohol.
4 Shake the mixture: the more it sits, the more ink concentrate you get!

Alcohol Inks and Polymer Clay

1 Take half a teaspoon of powdered RIT dye and add six teaspoons of rubbing alcohol: the salt sits on the bottom, sludge-like. (Later, you can filter the salt out using a coffee filter, but this is time-consuming. The unfiltered salt will not affect the ink quality if you prefer to leave it in the bottom.)
2 Add your alcohol ink to a polymer clay (such as Premo Sculpey) and bake according to the manufacturer's instructions.

(N.B.: The liquid version of RIT dye does not mix. In order to counter that, add two teaspoons of water to the mixture. Commercial alcohol inks definitely work better on polymer than the DIY versions. I highly recommend Adirondack Ranger inks for use on polymer clay; however, if you are on a tight budget, this formula will work, although your colors may be more muted than desired. For all dilutions, be sure to keep shaking the bottle before and between each use, just to keep the alcohol and dye from separating.)

DIY Masking Fluid/Frisket for Alcohol Ink or Watercolor Painting

Ingredients

- Cheap rubber cement
- Acetone or nail polish remover, or even better Citra Solv, since it is non-toxic. *(N.B.: If using acetone or nail polish remover, make sure that you are in a well-ventilated area.)*

Process

1 Empty about a third of the rubber cement out of the jar to make room for the nail polish remover, acetone, or Citra Solv. There should be at least 1″ to 1.5″ of space at the top of the jar. Next, put your remover of choice into the jar, replace the lid, and shake until thoroughly mixed. Check the consistency. Add more remover and repeat if necessary. *(N.B.: Add the remover a little at a time. You can always add more, but if you add too much straight away, the glue will be ruined.)*
2 After mixing, the rubber cement should have a thin, runny consistency, but not watery. It needs to be thin enough to spread easily, but thick enough to protect the paper or substrate.

3 To use the masking fluid, simply apply it to any areas that you want to protect using an old brush that you don't mind ruining, or clean with Citra Solv, acetone, or the like after use. (I prefer placing the rubber cement in a gutta applicator bottle with varying tips, available at Dharma Trading Co. (www.dharmatradingcompany.com), which allows me to control the output of the masking fluid.) Be sure to apply a nice, thick coat. You may want to apply a second coat after it dries to ensure that all of your substrate is covered.
4 Set it aside to dry thoroughly before proceeding. When the rubber cement mixture is totally dry, the surface will appear matte. Gently touch it with your finger to make sure that it is dry before you paint over it.
5 Once the paint has completely dried, take a small piece of masking tape and gently rub the sticky side of the tape on the dried rubber cement. It will slowly begin pulling it up off the paper. Continue rubbing the tape on the paper until all of the masking fluid is removed. You can also use an eraser to remove the masking fluid, but tape won't damage the surface of the paper. That's it! Continue your painting and either add ink to the masked area, or leave it white.

(N.B.: Having a frisket or masking fluid for alcohol ink painting is critical to maintain white space in your paintings.)

Methods for Using Alcohol Inks: Specialty Papers with Stencils, Glass, Ceramic, and Polymer Clay

Obviously, the methods for using alcohol inks are as diverse as the substrate and your imagination. You can use stencils on a specialty paper such as YUPO Synthetic paper (Figure 3.13), and placing freezer paper or parchment paper underneath the YUPO Synthetic paper will also yield a beautiful byproduct. Figure 3.14 shows a lovely example of alcohol ink used on polymer clay to make incredible jewelry by the Israeli artist, Iris Mishly. More of her work can be seen at PolyPedia Online Express (www.polypediaonlineexpress.com).

While you can use straws, Q-tips, cotton balls, and similar tools to manipulate the alcohol inks (Adirondack Ranger, a superior brand, or the DIY kind), the Tim Holtz Waterbrush is an essential tool for controlling alcohol inks. Available in two tip sizes (detail or wide-brush), these brushes can be used for a variety of creative painting techniques. Dab the water-filled brush with alcohol-based inks and the controlled water delivery system allows for optimal paint mixing and surface coverage, whether on YUPO papers, ceramic, glass, fabric, or polymer clay. For more on using alcohol inks on non-porous surfaces, Cathy Taylor's *Pigments of Your Imagination: Creating with Alcohol Inks* (2015) is an excellent resource and stunningly illustrated with works from numerous guest artists.

Figure 3.13 A heron created by the author, using masking fluid, alcohol inks, alcohol blenders, and inks.

Figure 3.14 Alcohol ink on polymer clay by artist Iris Mishly. (Printed with permission.)

Population Benefits and Contraindications

Obviously, using alcohol inks and the products described within this section requires intermediate skill levels and a developmental stage of pubescent/adolescent and up. But for patients who have a moderate degree of flexibility, artistic desire, and openness to experimentation, alcohol inks can be particularly freeing. While using the Tim Holtz Waterbrush gives a modicum of control, using less controlling methods (such as blowing through a straw to get abstract effects) works especially well with populations that are particularly challenged by control issues and/or obsessive-compulsive disorders (OCD). In small doses, when using alcohol inks on various surfaces and substrates, desensitization of OCD tendencies can occur. Therefore, I highly recommend experimenting with these materials to move toward both spontaneity and building self-esteem in populations that may struggle with these aforementioned issues. Furthermore, even if your patients become frustrated by alcohol ink media, discussion around such an event can be quite fruitful as one moves toward eradication of feelings associated with the lack of control.

Watercolor and Acrylic Paints

Watercolor Paint

While watercolor paint is a very portable medium to work with, it can often be quite frustrating for a beginning painter. Having been schooled in the traditional way of watercolor painting, I have always shunned friskets or masking fluids. *(N.B.: For those patients who crave optimal control, having masking fluids and friskets available can be useful. Masking fluids prevent the paper from absorbing color. You can use a watercolor mask before you apply a wash to protect areas that you want to remain white (such as clouds). Peel away the mask when it is no longer needed. Most masking fluids use natural latex or a synthetic compound with very similar characteristics. They may contain an artificial colorant so that you can easily identify the areas that you have masked. In the preceding section on alcohol inks, I provided a DIY recipe for making homemade masking fluids.)*

In classic watercolor painting, the white of the paper is your true white; there is no white paint in conventional methods of applying watercolor and so the build-up (if you prefer layers) can take hours. Figure 3.15 illustrates an example that I created using this build-up method. This build-up of layers, to create a translucent yet realistic effect, took me over 75 hours – a labor of love, since I was creating this watercolor for my brother's birthday.

However, this medium can work for a variety of patients (with or without masking fluids). In one case, I used watercolor exclusively as a preemptive

Figure 3.15 A watercolor painting of my brother, Len, created using the build-up method.

exercise and then moved on to acrylic paint with a 71-year-old stroke survivor, Bob, who had sustained a massive left-middle hemisphere CVA in 1997, resulting in Broca's aphasia, severe apraxia, and right-side hemiparesis. His language was often characterized by severe word retrieval difficulties. (A more extensive account of my work with Bob can be found in a previous publication: Horovitz, 2005.)

Bob's primary mode of communication was speech – yet it was emitted slowly and at low volume, and produced with great effort. His speech production was often inaccurate due to apraxia. His strengths were good auditory comprehension and a wry sense of humor. In addition, he attended to detail and had an able, working memory. He also displayed the ability to write if presented with a word to copy. However, he was extremely frustrated by his inability to use his dominant hand in art therapy. While initially he was seen for four months in a men's group, eventually I saw him for individual art therapy sessions and while doing so, for one year, I tied up my dominant hand with a bandana so we were both on equal footing. This truly encouraged Bob and, in time, his work moved from the developmental gang art stage (approximately 9–12 years old (Lowenfeld & Brittain, 1975)) to the adult, artistic stage of development (Horovitz, 2014). Figure 3.16 shows a sample of his progress using watercolor paints at that time. The image on the left of Figure 3.16 is of a watercolor painting that he signed and gave to me. A few months later, he created the breathtaking watercolor still life shown in the image on the right. Later, as he progressed, he was able to master the medium and use the white of the paper more readily (Figure 3.17).

Figure 3.16 Watercolor paintings created by Bob, a 71-year-old stroke survivor. Note the advancement from beginning (the flowers on the left) to months later (the still life with corn, tomatoes, and plant on the right). (Printed with permission.)

Figure 3.17 Another watercolor image created by Bob: a card for his wife. (Printed with permission.)

Another case of developmental gain using watercolor was my work with R, an 11-year-old African-American boy. R had been electively mute for two years since witnessing his father being bludgeoned to death in a bar room brawl. After several months of art therapy, this young boy not only blossomed creatively but also made enormous cognitive, emotional, and developmental gains. He began conversing again, and was able to leave day-care treatment and return at full scholarship to a technology middle school. This young man later went on to be an art teacher in the public school system.

Figure 3.18 Top: R's work at the beginning of treatment. Bottom: R's stunning watercolor of a woman after several months of art therapy. (Printed with permission.)

(N.B.: While watercolor paints can range from cake to tube varieties, products such as Winsor & Newton watercolors can be prohibitively expensive for the art therapist; however, the watercolor images created by these patients were done with Grumbacher watercolor pan sets. Furthermore, these images were done on drawing paper, rather than watercolor paper. While watercolor paper is preferable and acid-free, it can be quite dear depending on the brand.)

Population Benefits and Contraindications

As stated before, working with watercolor paint requires a modicum of patience, lest it become muddy and overworked. But I have used this medium with all ages (3–96) and a variety of populations. I would highly recommend using this medium and offering the masking fluids if the patient becomes frustrated by the inability to use white in color mixing. I highly recommend experimenting with the watercolor materials to move toward both spontaneity and building self-esteem in populations that may struggle with these aforementioned issues.

Acrylic Paint

Acrylic paint is a fast-drying paint made of pigment suspended in acrylic polymer emulsion. Acrylic paints are water-soluble, become water-resistant when dry, dry quickly, and with varnishes can produce effects that mirror oil paintings. A master of this technique is Kathy Calderwood (www.kathycalderwood.com).

It is assumed that for color mixing, in any medium using color, art therapists are familiar with the rudimentary mixing of the color wheel. Figure 3.19 illustrates primary colors (red, yellow, and blue), secondary colors (shades made by combining primary colors: orange, violet and green), and tertiary colors (shades made by combining secondary colors). However, this color wheel is wholly different from digital graphics and/or photography, which will be covered in Chapter 4.

Below are some suggested acrylic paint products:

- Golden Paints, Liquitex, Pébéo (my personal favorites), Winsor & Newton, etc.)
- generic paints (such as Blicks) from my preferred art store vendor, Dick Blick Art Materials (www.dickblick.com).

But here is a little secret: you can actually purchase pint-sized (or larger) cans of acrylic paint (better known as house interior and/or exterior paint) from your local hardware store and it saves you a ton of money! And you can mix your own colors beyond the primary, secondary, and tertiary colors. But if you do not want to go to the hassle of deploying paint from pint-sized cans, for the money, Blicks paints are excellent quality with a long shelf life. So for your average studio, I would invest in these.

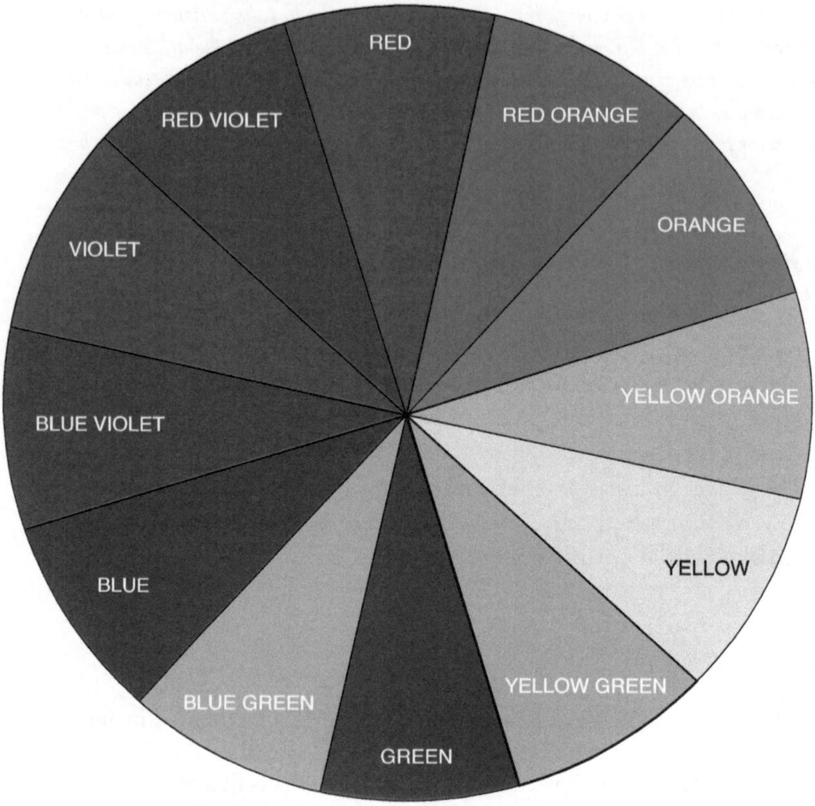

Figure 3.19 The basic color wheel: primary, secondary, and tertiary colors, provided by Monster Marketing Partners (www. monstermarketingpartners.com). (Printed with permission.)

A time-saving trick (which I learned from Edith Kramer) is to dump the primary color paints, two whites for mixing, and one black into muffin tins. *(Hint: You can place the paints in the freezer (preferably covered) and then pin-prick the skin that forms over the top to use for your next session.)* I upgraded Kramer's idea by taking my Tupperware containers, placing those in the muffin tins, filling them with paint and then leaving them stored and ready to go in my studio. (Short of this, you could use empty baby food containers to do the same thing, but I prefer Tupperware containers since they are not glass.) Styrofoam trays (recycled from your local grocery store) make excellent palettes. While one might prefer foam trays when working with young children, I prefer to use a white dinner-sized dish for my palette (available at your local dollar store). These can be washed and reused *ad infinitum*.

Because acrylic paints are so fast-drying, they are a step up from poster or tempera paints and preferable to use with adolescents and adults. Bob, the 71-year-old stroke survivor mentioned earlier in the watercolor section, gradually became interested in canvas painting as his skills improved. Figure 3.20

Figure 3.20 Left: Bob painting his acrylic still life. Right: The finished painting. (Printed with permission.)

shows an example of Bob painting from a still life (which I had set up in our studio) and the finished acrylic painting on the right.

Figure 3.21 shows another example, of an acrylic painting by an 11-year-old boy dually diagnosed with neurocognitive and conduct disorder. In this instance, the Superman and Supergirl paintings aided the young boy in working on self-esteem issues.

Sealing your paint products can offer a luster or sheen that mirrors the quality that one can get from oil paints. Kathy Calderwood, the excellent painter mentioned earlier, layers her paints with Blair Varnish Gloss spray. By applying several layers of the gloss finish, you can achieve a marvelous luster. (Naturally, this should be done outside or in a well-ventilated area.) *(N.B.: You do not need to varnish or seal acrylic paintings but this extra step can certainly enhance the final image.)*

Figure 3.21 An acrylic painting done by an 11-year-old boy dually diagnosed with neurocognitive and conduct disorder. (Printed with permission.)

Population Benefits and Contraindications

You can use acrylic paint with all ages (3–96) and a variety of populations, but I would recommend using it with patients aged pre-adolescent and up. Acrylic paints can be used on a variety of surfaces (not just canvas sheets, boards, or stretched canvases). I have used acrylic paints on Masonite (pre-painted with gesso), wood, papier-mâché, clay, metal, etc. Acrylic paint is an extremely versatile medium that can be easily stored and used to finish and enhance a variety of materials. Naturally, care must be taken when using these products to be in a well-ventilated area, especially if sealing with Mod-Podge, Blair Varnish Gloss, or like products. *Furthermore, these products may be contraindicated with a dementia population. In the past, I have actually had dementia patients attempt to eat acrylic paint. With that population, it is advised to use water and food coloring in case the paint is swallowed.*

Printmaking

Printmaking is the process of making artworks by printing, normally on paper. While printmaking normally covers the process of creating prints that have an element of originality, in recent years, printmaking has also incorporated photographic elements. Different from painting, printmaking generally assumes that there may be multiples of the same image, unless creating a monoprint. In this section, we will look at using both monoprints and traditional printmaking where multiples of the same design may result. In fact, it is even possible to get a print-off of a monoprint (one unique print, although some refer to this a "ghost" print). *(N.B.: Advanced methods of printmaking – etching, intaglio, aquatint, and lithography – will not be covered. The methods here will appeal to art therapy clinicians, rather than a fine arts crowd. Cyanotypes or blueprints as well as printing with gesso will be covered in Chapter 4.)* According to Dean (2016b), "even the most well-conceived and thoughtfully executed designs have an element of chance to them" (p. 254). Much is out of control but, as von Franz (1980) states, it is the response to the process/product that yields therapeutic benefit.

Basic Printmaking Materials Needed

- Method for printing (foam trays, E-Z Speedball Printing Plate, Gelli Arts Gel Printing Plates, linoleum plates, or Soft-Kut Printing Blocks are just some of the suggestions)
- Inking plates (see bottom image of Figure 3.22); can also be used to hook onto a table for cutting with linoleum block printing tools

- Cutting plate (see top image of Figure 3.22); these can be hand made from wood
- Brayers for inking (see bottom image of Figure 3.22)
- Various papers including rice paper for fine printing
- Water-based inks (including acrylic for Gelli Arts Gel Painting Plates)
- Newspaper and paper towels for clean-up.

Methods used by art therapists may include potato or vegetable printing (Weiss, 1976), linoleum block prints, foam-tray printing, cardboard/collograph prints (or relief printmaking), and Gelli Arts Gel Printing Plates, which can yield monoprints that involve layering. While Plexiglas plates can also be loaded with acrylic or tempera paint, the plasticity of Gelli Arts Gel Painting Plates encourages drying of layers between the final pull for the monoprint. Plexiglass cannot yield this effect and generally requires oil paint to do so. For that reason, I consider plexiglass plates for monoprinting to be rather old school. While Gelli Arts Gel Printing Plates are expensive, they are reusable and well worth the investment. But let's first look at foam-plate printing because of its ease of use and availability.

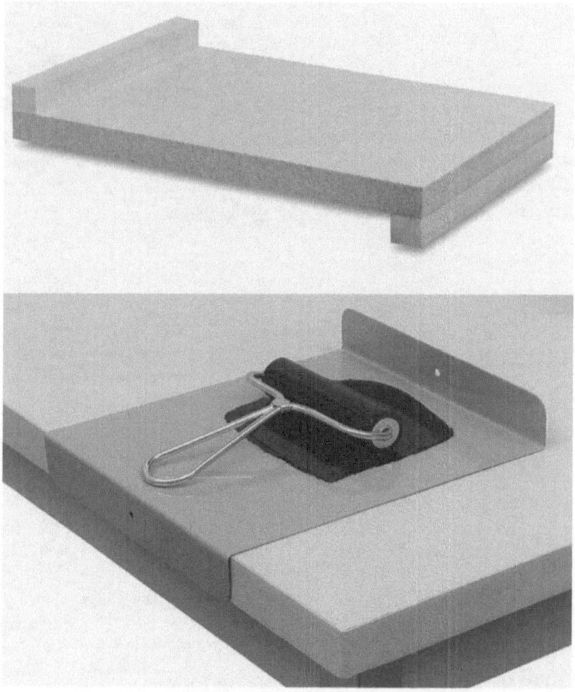

Figure 3.22 Top: A wooden cutting plate. Bottom: An inking plate with a brayer and ink.

Foam Plates

Foam plates are available at your local grocery store as they sit underneath meat, fish, chicken, vegetables, fruit, etc. While a foam plate also makes a great painting palette, you can cut off the tray-like sides, wash it, dry it, and then simply take a pencil to draw into the material. It is very easy to do and takes very little hand strength, which is a plus when working with physically challenged populations (stroke survivors, cerebral palsy patients, Parkinson's patients, etc.). Using water-based printing ink (Speedball, Jacquard, or Blick, or a like product), the trays can be loaded with a brayer of the inks and then paper can simply be placed atop the foam tray. Next, gingerly rub the paper with a wooden spoon, gently lift off the paper, and the yield is excellent. (You can also use a separate clean brayer for imprinting the ink onto the paper.)

The beauty of making multiple prints is that the maker has numerous copies of his/her artwork to give away or use in other ways, such as collage. Below are two examples of foam-plate printmaking created by two different patients: one with cerebral palsy (Figure 3.23) and another with mild neurocognitive disorder (Figure 3.24). As you can see, the results are quite good!

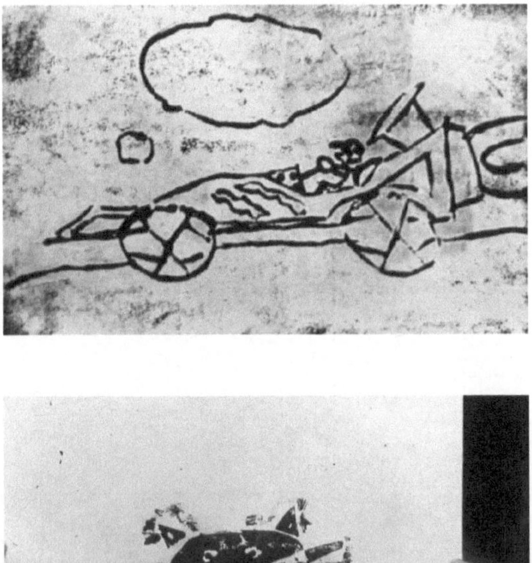

Figure 3.23 A foam-plate print created by a 9-year-old patient with cerebral palsy. (Printed with permission.)

Figure 3.24 A foam-plate print created by a 12-year-old patient with mild neurocognitive disorder. (Printed with permission.)

Collograph / Cardboard Prints

Instead of being reductionistic, like the foam plates where you are cutting away material, with the collograph/cardboard method you are building up materials. The printmaking process involves a substrate (such as cardboard, paperboard, or wood) where the print is built up. Figure 3.25 shows two 12-year-old girls diagnosed with attention deficit disorder (ADD) involved in the process of making the cardboard plate (top left), trying it out in pencil (top right), and then the final print rubbed with crayons (bottom). (Clearly, they attended to this activity well, which took several sessions to complete.) Again, this can be done with recyclable boxes, cereal boxes, and just about anything where you can affix one surface to another.

Figure 3.25 12-year-old girls with ADD creating a cardboard print.

Soft-Kut Block Plates and Linoleum Plates

While the surfaces are different, "Soft-Kut" implying that little pressure is needed, both linoleum block plates and the Soft-Kut Block Plates can be used with linoleum-cutting tools. These cutting tools come in a variety of sizes and quality. My personal favorites for working with an art therapy population is the Speedball Linoleum Cutter, which comes with six different cutting tools (small V, large V, small U gouge, square gouge, large U gouge, and the knife). (These cutting tools are designed to reside inside the tool itself. The back cap comes off and safely holds the unused cutting tools.)

The Soft-Kut Block Plates and linoleum plates work especially well for patients who have a modicum of skill and artistic predilection. While one might be cautious about offering these tools to patients who are more aggressive in nature, I have used these items one-on-one with oppositional defiant and aggressive individuals with much success. So, I wouldn't necessarily rule the linoleum cutters out. Just proceed with caution and take your cues from observation. This will quickly inform you as to what type of individual would benefit from working with these materials. Personally, I love the Soft-Kut Block Plates and linoleum plates because they are more advanced and can even be used to print on fabric using inks designed for fabric printing. (Again, Speedball makes an excellent fabric block printing ink for that purpose and it does not wash out once dried.) Furthermore, if you add elements of collage to items such as my example (bottom print in Figure 3.26), then each print can be a unique item. Mariann Johansen-Ellis, an extraordinary print artist from Denmark, provided me with a

Figure 3.26 Top: An example of a linoleum block print. Bottom: A print by the author.

Figure 3.27 "Sunday Lunch," a linoleum block print by artist Mariann Johansen-Ellis. (Printed with permission.)

wonderful example of her linoleum block print work, "Sunday Lunch" (Figure 3.27). Her fabulous artwork can be seen at www.mariannjohansen-ellis.com.

Gelli Arts Gel Printing Plates

Gelli Arts Gel Printing Plates can be reused and cleaned up with hand sanitizer. This product is a great tool for the mobile art therapist without access to a sink, which can often be a difficulty when working with patients. The beauty of Gelli Arts Gel Printing Plates is that they can be stored in their plastic housing; they can be layered with multiple colors; and stencils, plastic paper, bubble wrap, and doilies can be utilized to create interesting textures. This very exciting product can yield some stunning results in less than a session and allows for experimentation, freeing up the most rigid of patients. Because the nature of the final print can be so unpredictable, generally this method works well with any age and population. One only needs the Gelli Arts Gel Printing Plate (which comes in a variety of shapes, including round!), a brayer, and a willingness to experiment. Figure 3.28 includes examples from an adult artist, which involved ginkgo leaf and fern stencils and layering acrylic paints before pulling the final prints. One can see how diverse the results can be, using a modicum of experimentation.

Figure 3.28 Top left: Gelli Arts Gel Printing Plate housing. Top right: A gel plate. Middle right and bottom left: Examples created by an adult artist. (Printed with permission.)

Population Benefits and Contraindications

Printmaking is a wonderful medium that allows for a wide variety of experimentation and use with several populations. Depending on the type of printing plate employed, this medium can be used with multiple populations (physically and cognitively challenged) as well as those with emotional disturbances. Care must be taken when working with dually diagnosed populations that the proper product is used. As stated in this section, when one is working with aggressive, acting-out individuals (such as those with antisocial personality disorder), linoleum block printing tools might be forgone for foam plates, cardboard plates, or Gelli Arts Gel Printing Plates, since these particular printmaking methods are easier to use and do not involve tools that might cut the individual and/or be used to harm someone else. While I have used Speedball Linoleum Cutters with patients with neurocognitive disorders and conduct disorder personalities, as stated before, it is best to use these cutters in a one-on-one situation, where you can keep your eye on the tools and the individual. More will be stated about this in Chapter 4, as well as about the next medium we will cover, clay.

Clay

Admittedly, of all media, clay is my favorite. There are a variety of reasons: its plasticity and forgiveness if you make a mistake, its nature (liquids, glazes, slips, and solids; earthenware, stoneware, and porcelain), its magical transformation (pliable, greenware, bisque-fired, and glazed), and its ability to transcend into fine art with almost any population. I also hold a place near to my heart for this medium because I first discovered (age 6) that I could sculpt anything I imagined from visualizing it in my mind; unfortunately, with two-dimensional applications, if the image is to be realistic in nature, I need a source for rendering. For artists, this ability can vary widely. Believe me, I have canvassed many artists about their abilities to render in both two- and three-dimensional materials and it is not the same for all.

Nonetheless, because the material is often manipulated with sharp tools, the art therapist needs to be extremely mindful when using such tools. While they can yield fabulous results, as will be seen in the examples in this section, they can also be dangerous in the hands of explosive personalities. Therefore, this would not be my first choice of material when first meeting a patient since engagement with potential weapons can unleash aggressive and regressive tendencies. Therefore, it is highly advisable that the therapist has a working idea of the patient's history and proceeds with caution.

But next, let's look at clay's properties and its wide applications in art therapy and psychotherapy. According to Sholt and Gavron (2006), "Many advocate the therapeutic potential of clay as a tool for advancing therapeutic processes in individual and group therapies . . . while others . . . ascribe to clay-work's diagnostic qualities in family and individual therapies" (p. 66). Moreover, Sholt and Gavron highlighted the aspect of making something concrete from a lump of clay, which then symbolically becomes a metaphor of the patient's inner world. Indeed, they likened this experience to "alchemy" allowing for both construction and deconstruction and thus enabling a psychic change in the individual and the material (p. 68). Henley (2002) also discussed this in his seminal text when he investigated the subject of clay and object loss.

In sum, clay-work involves both the body and the mind (via the physical action of manipulating the clay and via the mental engagement of modeling and observation). Because of its three-dimensional quality, clay encourages the integration of emotions, memories, and fantasies from different levels of consciousness. The potential intensity of clay-work in bringing up such unconscious material and amplifying the personal meaning of a symbol (Kagin & Lusebrink, 1978) can lead to premature disclosure, especially in the treatment of traumatic issues. Because of its inherent capacity to release such affect, caution should be applied in the use of clay-work in art therapy and in psychotherapy. Considering the need to proceed with caution, a short case will be presented in which disclosure during an assessment of the clay subtest of the Cognitive Art Therapy Assessment (CATA) (Horovitz, 2014) yielded information that had not previously been presented by the IP. Because of this, the objectives and treatment team goals of this patient were re-formulated after the reveal of his clay artwork.

The Case of W

In this very complicated case, we will see how the CATA yielded poignant information about W and his dissociation as expressed via the clay. But in order to understand how this material unleashed W's dissociative state, first a look at his background will be helpful. W's genogram (Figure 3.29) presents a visual map of his case. Familial information and the reasons for referral will elucidate the picture.

During the CATA clay subtest, W was very involved with the clay medium and while much information resulted from the other CATA subtests (achromatic pencil and paint), his response to using the clay led to a verbal outpouring of information that had not been revealed in earlier assessment batteries (the HTP (House–Tree–Person) test, the KFD (Kinetic Family Drawing), or the SDT (Silver Drawing Test)). For these reasons, because he was so invested, I allowed W to create a second response. But looking at the first clay response (Figure 3.30), W's creation of just a clay mouth with teeth and tongue suggested oral, aggressive preoccupation and a concomitant identification with the aggressor (perhaps a sexual predator, in this case). Indeed, his verbal response that he "felt taken advantage of" was the first index alluding to the sexual abuse at the hands of his perpetrators, his paternal uncles. Still later, when he created his second clay response (Figure 3.31), he stated that the image's head was an "explosive volcano" (suggesting volatile emotive feelings). Looking carefully at the second head placed atop the larger head shown in

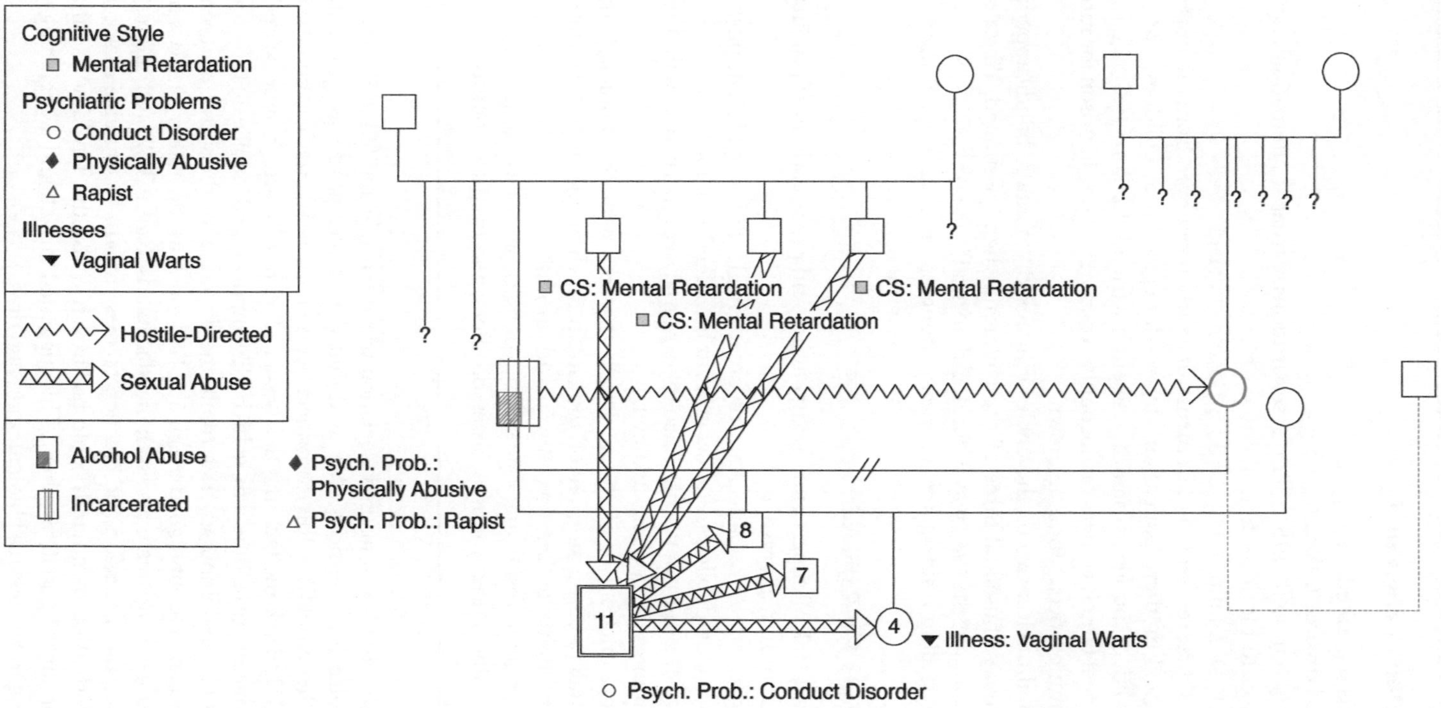

Figure 3.29 W's genogram. (Printed with permission.)

Familial Background

Parents separated, W's age 2
Parents divorced, W's age 6.5
Parents reunited with multiple separations, physical altercations, and moves to Florida – four in one year
Age 11, W monitored by CPS for possible neglect
Age 13, first residential placement; all children removed from the home
Biological mother: Caucasian, divorced, neglectful of children, unemployed, on public assistance; current boyfriend slumlord
Biological father: Caucasian, alcoholic, re-married; was in prison for rape of minor; occupation unknown
Paternal uncles: two of the uncles diagnosed "mentally handicapped;" sexually abused all three of the children; when questioned, W stated he thought the "sex was natural and normal"
Siblings: all in residential placement; youngest sister has vaginal warts

Reasons for Referral

Neglect, lack of supervision, sexual abuse and perpetration with siblings and cousins, aggressive
Biological mother: Caucasian, divorced, neglectful of children, unemployed, on public assistance; current boyfriend slumlord
Biological father: Caucasian, alcoholic, re-married; was in prison for rape of minor; occupation unknown
Paternal uncles: two of the uncles diagnosed "mentally handicapped;" sexually abused all three of the children; when questioned, W stated he thought the "sex was natural and normal"
Siblings: all in residential placement; youngest sister has vaginal warts
W sexually abused youngest sister, brothers, and his male cousins.

Figure 3.31, the first hint of dissociation was ostensible and led to the direction for the subsequent sessions. W stated that the smaller head was "just hanging out," further amplifying this disconnect between the head (intellect) and the body (emotion). Indeed, the fact that this was just "all head" further underscored W's disembodiment, detachment from his bodily impulses, and inability to monitor and check his libidinal impulses. As a result, the direction for the subsequent sessions led to discussion around good touch and bad touch as the author cast W's hands via plaster gauze to create his silver, metallic hands (Figure 3.32). (Of interest was that during the discussion and creation of these hands, W was able to articulate that he wished his own hands could be "frozen" ("like the Tin Man") so that he could not harm himself or others. This suggested growth and a beginning sense of wanting to harness his libidinal urges and drive.)

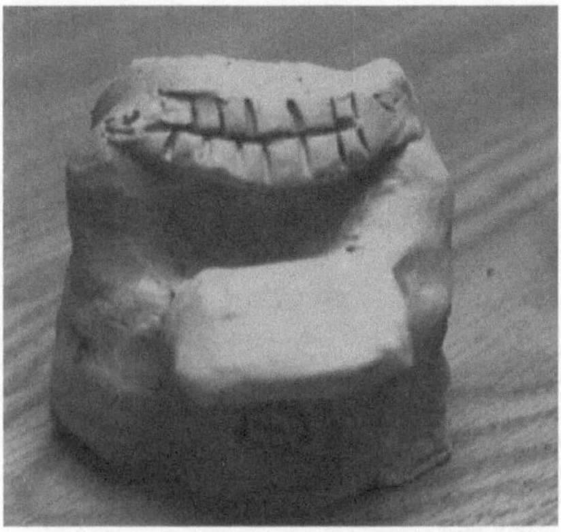

Figure 3.30 W's CATA clay response #1. (Printed with permission.)

Figure 3.31 W's CATA clay response #2. (Printed with permission.)

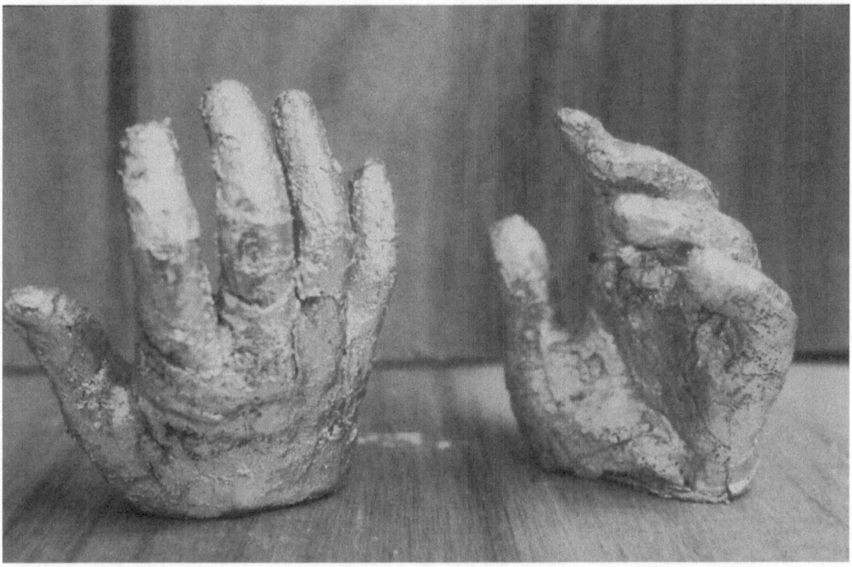

Figure 3.32 W's plaster gauze hands, painted silver. (Printed with permission.)

The Case of E

In this next case of E, we will see how a skilled Deaf adolescent was able to use the clay medium for self-expression and communication with this clinician. Her genogram is shown in Figure 3.33. Analyzing a family's system via its communication style is fundamental to family therapy. With the Deaf population, this becomes crucial. As mentioned in Chapter 2, modes of communication employed by family members vary and the range of language systems may be

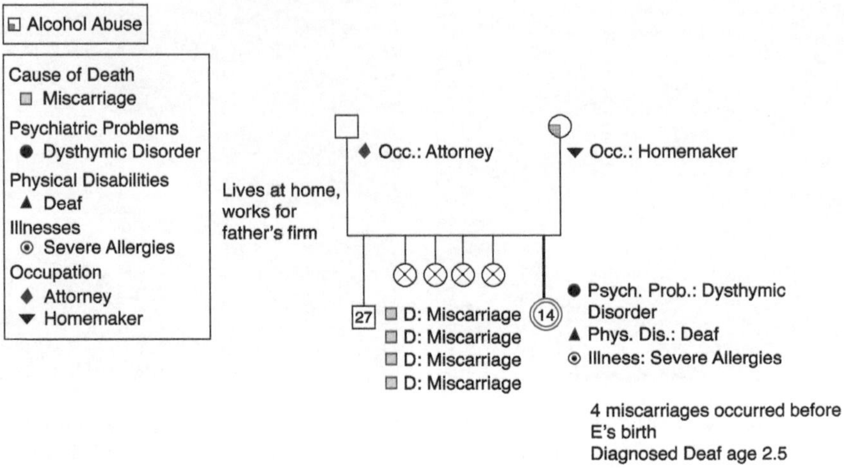

Figure 3.33 E's genogram. (Printed with permission.)

expansive, circumscribed, bimodal, or virtually absent (Horovitz-Darby, 1991). For the Deaf child, visual information constitutes inner language. Without expression or a way to communicate this language, the Deaf child becomes trapped, isolated from his/her family system (Horovitz, 2007).

Timeline and History

Prior to E's birth, there had been four miscarriages, and her mother lost 30 pounds during the pregnancy with E. She also had the Asian flu during part of the pregnancy; her mother was 40 years old at the time of E's birth.

Pregnancy was described as difficult. E's health at birth was extremely poor; E's lungs filled with foreign matter prior to birth and it was uncertain whether or not she would live the first four days after birth. E was transferred to a neonatal unit and then discharged ten days later to home.

E was bottle fed and weaned at age 6 months; she was slow to eat solid foods.

Developmentally, E was somewhat delayed – she crawled but did not walk until age 1.5; she was toilet trained during the day by age 4, but not at night until age 9.

Hearing loss was discovered at age 2.5.

Age 6, E was hospitalized for minor surgery for a thyroglossal cyst; she had a tonsillectomy and adenoidectomy at the same time period. She required myringotomies bilaterally due to upper respiratory infection and otitis.

Sever's disease, involving the heel of her left foot, was discovered at age 12. A plastic heel cup was provided to distribute force equally.

She is allergic to some perfumes and wool; she is currently on no medication, although from 3.5 to 7 years old she received Ritalin for hyperactivity. According to her mother, E was considered to be learning disabled (LD).

There were numerous ear infections from swimming.

Age 3–5, E attended a program for the Deaf. Yet, she was mainstreamed by kindergarten.

Age 6–9, E was in LD classes; at age 9, her hearing ability decreased and she qualified for a class for the hearing impaired. This was described as a "miserable time" for E. She did not use signs before age 9 to communicate and all communication was performed orally. E was encouraged to talk but none of her classmates could talk and in fact were quite cruel to her. As a result, E forged friendships with hearing children.

At age 13, she was placed at an inpatient hospital for dysthymic disorder, mixed specific developmental disorder, and bilateral hearing impairment. In addition, it was reported that she was both withdrawn and intermittently explosive. When frustrated, she would become destructive, once throwing a rocking chair and resorting to head banging.

E has confusion as to where she fits – she states a preference for operating within the hearing world, yet feels "different."

This case was discussed in great depth in an earlier book (Horovitz, 2007). There were approximately 42 individual art therapy sessions. E's discourse was emotionally laden, continuous, and bordered on hysterical, histrionic patter. Topics included her fixation on anorexia nervosa (she began struggling with her eating during her residential treatment), projections of other family members' "issues" (as opposed to her own), continuous fantasies about a "twin sister," and being discharged from treatment. (The twin sister might be harbored guilt around the miscarriages preceding her birth.) Since she benefited from art therapy, the frequency of her sessions was increased to three times a week after the first 13 sessions. This was just the medicinal ticket she needed.

E was finally able to accept her inability to change the familial patterns of behavior. Her artwork blossomed; I secured a scholarship for her to attend the Memorial Art Gallery (the University of Rochester museum) for Saturday classes; and she began to make active plans to work toward acceptance at NTID (the National Technical Institute for the Deaf) or Gallaudet University as an art student. Furthermore, she entered a contest and won an Honorable Mention for her fabulous piece below, which she aptly named "The Missing Piece." E was able to articulate her struggles with "fitting into" her familial paradigm since her deafness left her feeling both isolated from the family system and a "misfit." She stated that if only her family could understand her language, perhaps she would not feel like an outcast and the differences might be mended. Figure 3.34 shows the stunning example that E created out of clay that illustrated her dilemma.

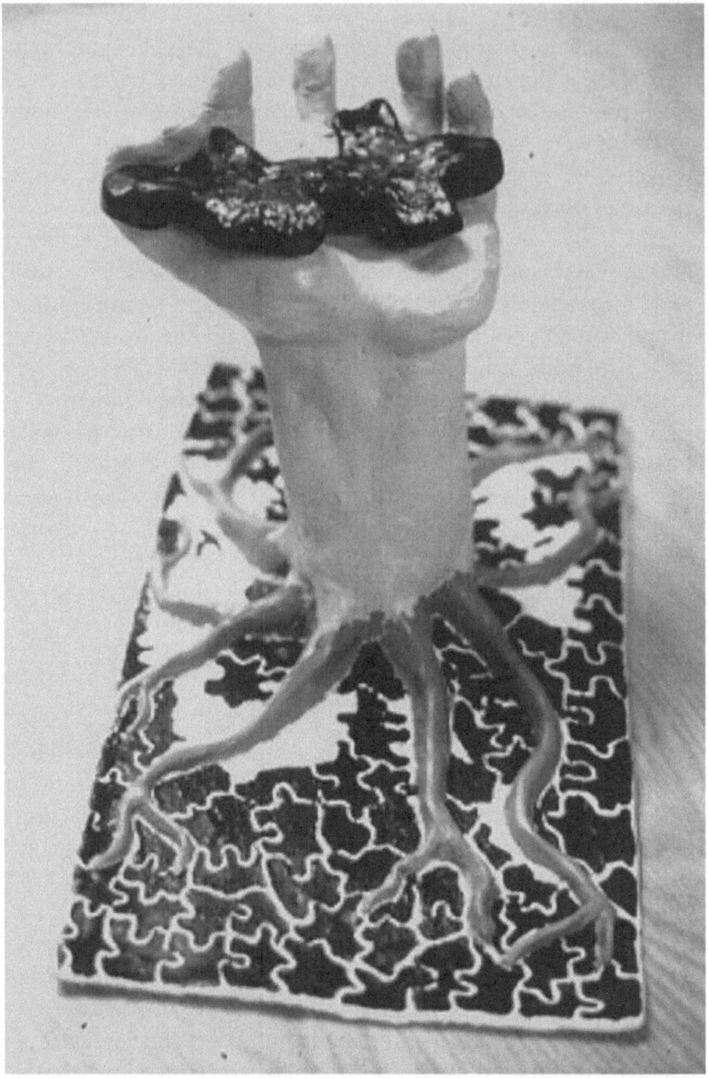

Figure 3.34 E's artwork entitled "The Missing Piece." (Printed with permission.)

While this could be analyzed for multiple meanings, the tree-like hand creates a formidable stand-in for the communication that E so desperately sought. *(N.B.: The family had been approached numerous times to participate in family art therapy sessions, but the response to this treatment request was sadly ignored by E's nuclear family system.)* Considering that the Deaf use their hands as a primary means of communication, this piece is all the more striking. Clearly, the clay had aided E in both creative and self-expression, which led to the union of emotions, memories, and neuro-processing around familial patterns.

Population Benefits and Contraindications

While clay can be used with populations of any age, care should be taken when introducing this medium since it has the capacity to foster both aggression and regression. Therefore, if you are working (for example) with a patient with dementia, he/she should be watched carefully since some dementia patients are prone to eating their materials. Furthermore, clay is often manipulated with sharp tools, and therefore the art therapist needs to be extremely mindful when using such tools with patients who have a history of aggression. Care must be taken when working with dually diagnosed populations that the proper medium is used. As stated in this section, when one is working with aggressive, acting-out individuals, once a therapeutic relationship has been established, the clay can result in formidable expression, cathartic release, and purposeful imagery. Furthermore, its inherent pliability and "forgiveness" as a medium allow for reworking the imagery as well as the emotional experiences tied to the material. Its three-dimensional quality is suited to all ages and in fact can yield great artistic and emotive expression.

References

Brannigan, G., & Decker, S. (2003). *Bender-Gestalt II: Bender visual-motor gestalt test: Examiner's manual* (2nd Ed.). Itasca, IL: The Riverside Publishing Company.

Buck, J. (1948). The H-T-P technique, a qualitative and quantitative scoring method. *Journal of Clinical Psychology Monograph Supplement, 4*(4), 317–390.

Dean, M. L. (2016a). *Using art media in psychotherapy: Bringing the power of creativity into the practice.* New York, NY: Routledge.

Dean, M. L. (2016b). Printmaking: Reflective and receptive impressions in the therapeutic process. In D. E. Gussak & M. L. Rosal (Eds.), *The Wiley handbook of art therapy* (pp. 171–179). Malden, MA: John Wiley & Sons, Ltd.

Dissanyake, E. (1992). *Homo aestheticus: Where art comes from and why*. New York, NY: Free Press.

Gantt, L., & Tabone, C. (1998). *The Formal Elements Art Therapy Scale: The rating manual.* Morgantown, WV: Gargoyle Press.

Hammer, E. F. (1980). *The clinical application of projective drawings* (6th Ed.). Springfield, IL: Charles C. Thomas.

Henley, D. (2002). *Clayworks in art therapy: Playing the sacred circle.* Philadelphia, PA: Jessica Kingsley.

Hinz, L. (2016). Media considerations in art therapy: Directions for future research. In D. E. Gussak & M. L. Rosal (Eds.), *The Wiley handbook of art therapy* (pp. 135–145). Malden, MA: John Wiley & Sons, Ltd.

Horovitz, E. G. (1991). Family art therapy within a Deaf system. *Arts in Psychotherapy, 18*, 257–261.

Horovitz, E. G. (1999). *A leap of faith: The call to art.* Springfield, IL: Charles C. Thomas.

Horovitz, E. G. (2005). *Art therapy as witness: A sacred guide.* Springfield, IL: Charles C. Thomas.

Horovitz, E. G. (Ed.). (2007). *Visually speaking: Art therapy and the Deaf.* Springfield, IL: Charles C. Thomas.

Horovitz, E. G. (2011). *Digital image transfer: Creating art with your photography*. New York, NY: Sterling Publishers.

Horovitz, E. G. (Ed.). (2014). *The art therapists' primer: A clinical guide to writing assessments, diagnosis, and treatment* (2nd Ed.). Springfield, IL: Charles C. Thomas.

Horovitz, E. G. (2016). Photography as therapy: Through academic and clinical explorations. In D. E. Gussak & M. L. Rosal (Eds.), *The Wiley handbook of art therapy* (pp. 180–187). Malden, MA: John Wiley & Sons, Ltd.

Kagin, S. L., & Lusebrink, V. B. (1978). The expressive therapies continuum. *Art Psychotherapy, 5*(4), 171–180.

Kramer, E. (1975). *Art as therapy with children.* New York, NY: Schocken Books.

Landgarten, H. (1981). *Clinical art therapy: A comprehensive guide.* New York, NY: Bruner/Mazel.

Landgarten, H. (1993). *Magazine photo collage: A multicultural assessment and treatment technique.* New York, NY: Bruner/Mazel.

LenFim Studio. (2011, December 11). Edith Kramer: Art tells the truth. Retrieved March 30, 2016 from https://vimeo.com/33476299.

Lowenfeld, V., & Brittain, W. L. (1975). *Creative and mental growth* (6th Ed.). New York, NY: Macmillan.

Machover, K. (1949). *Personality projection in the drawing of the human figure: A method of personality investigation.* Springfield, IL: Charles C. Thomas.

Piyasena, S., & Philp, B. (2014). *Just paint it!: The world's most enjoyable painting course. Ever!* Tunbridge Wells, Kent: Quarto Publishing.

Rubin, J. A. (1998). *Introduction to art therapy: Sources and resources.* New York, NY: Routledge.

Sholt, M., & Gavron, T. (2006). Therapeutic qualities of clay-work in art therapy and psychotherapy: A review. *Art Therapy: Journal of the American Art Therapy Association, 23*(2), 66–72.

Stallings, J. W. (2009). Collage as a therapeutic modality for reminiscence for people with dementia. *Art Therapy: Journal of the American Art Therapy Association, 27*(3), 136–140.

Stallings, J. W. (2016). Collage as an expressive medium in Art Therapy. In D. E. Gussak & M. L. Rosal (Eds.), *The Wiley handbook of art therapy* (pp. 163–170). Malden, MA: John Wiley & Sons, Ltd.

Taylor, C. (2015). *Pigments of your imagination: Creating with alcohol inks.* Atglen, PA: Schiffer Publishing, Ltd.

von Franz, M. L. (1980). *On divination and synchronicity: The psychological meaning of chance.* Toronto, ON: Inner City Books.

Weiss, P. (1976). *Simple printmaking.* New York, NY: Lothrop, Lee, & Shepard Co.

Websites

Dick Blick Art Materials: www.dickblick.com (Retrieved June 24, 2017).

Lani Gerrity Glanville: http://14secretsforahappyartistslife.blogspot.com/ (Retrieved June 8, 2017).

Mariann Johansen-Ellis: www.mariannjohansen-ellis.com (Retrieved June 8, 2017).

PolyPedia Online Express: www.polypediaonlineexpress.com (Retrieved June 8, 2017).

4 Advanced Materials and Techniques

Strategies and Case Studies

The hand is the tool of tools.

Aristotle, *On the Soul* (2006)

Introduction

Over the years, I have felt an obligation to expand and vary my artistic palette. The reasons are myriad. My son, Bryan, calculates my boredom with subject matters as a consequence of my "ever-curious" mind. Yet I differ: I have always felt that it was more than that. For me, widening the scope of materials beyond the "basics," as described in Chapter 3, is a responsibility both to my patients and my artistic self-inquiry. My obligation to my patients is to remain current. That is, my commitment to learning new artistic endeavors is analogous to research for the art therapist. It is my opinion that art therapy clinicians should be just as curious about art materials and byproducts as they are about researching the fields of art therapy, psychology, neurology, morphology, and any related areas of study. McNiff (1998) talked about this in his epic book, *Art-Based Research.* Knowing the ABCs of art materials should be a *given* for the art therapist, but reaching beyond the materials outlined in Chapter 3 is a commitment to lifelong learning. (Think of this as the CECs (Continuing Education Credits) or CEUs (Continuing Education Units) that one should constantly acquire.) It is no different than embracing the *DSM-5* or the *ICD-10* codes. It all matters. Therefore, I encourage the incipient or seasoned art therapist to think of this section as a "jumping-off" point.

Phototherapy Techniques

In 1992, when I engaged with professors in CUSeeMe (the acronym for Cornell University's online chat), there was a two-second delay in "streaming live" with fellow researchers. Today, that delay would be an embarrassment to any app. However, back then, it was a rare privilege to explore this potential talk-space on the internet; at that time, the World Wide Web (WWW) was pretty much in its infancy. Now, apps abound. But those were the days when Photoshop had just been released (February 2, 1990). On that day, the world and photography as I knew it were forever changed. And while I did not "throw out the baby with the bath water" (I still work with real film), combining both analog and digital platforms has afforded me the ability to combine traditional and new photography. Since then, I have employed a host of products to aid me in phototherapy techniques (Horovitz, 2011). I scoured the research and read the more historical texts of Krauss and Fryear (1983) and Fryear and Corbit (1992). But truly it wasn't until I read the work of Weiser (1993) that I really understood the phototherapy practices that I had been using. The beauty of phototherapy (which can be understood as a variety of ideologies that examine pictures of one's past to create pictures/photographs/sculptures/videos, etc. from one's current perspective) is that the inherent work has the "ability to immediately trigger memories, trigger affect, [and] put the client back into that feeling state" (Krauss, 1979) in a way that actually no other medium can. As an art therapy clinician, I have patients with complex etiologies of varying typology. Indeed, I have repeatedly witnessed the power of photographic images in accelerating recovery in unreachable patients. But from a historical viewpoint, it is indeed understandable. As Weiser suggests:

> We can only be aware of ourselves to the extent that we can self-reflect; our existence at any moment is a summary of selective memory and, within the distortive nature of that process, also a partial fiction created only by what we can know of ourselves and have introjected from others.
>
> (1993, p. 20)

If you want a more in-depth view of the kinds of methods that one can employ, feel free to read my earlier work (Horovitz, 2011) or my in-depth chapter in *The Wiley Handbook of Art Therapy* (Horovitz, 2016b). Here, I will briefly cover some of the exciting materials that one can use in the following section on phototherapy techniques.

Laser Printers versus Inkjet Printers

There are numerous ways of transferring images to substrates. Substrates can be loosely defined as anything that can receive the image that you wish to output. The machine that you use to produce your images is specific to the papers and desired output. (Some papers are made specifically for inkjet printers while others are made specifically for laser printers or photocopy machines.) Heat-based transfers (which use photocopy machines or laser printers) are essential for using acetone, Xylol, or Citra Solv to transfer your imagery onto wood, fabric, polymer clay, leather, or even metal surfaces. In this section on phototherapy and its applications, I will introduce just a few ways to use some of the techniques that I have employed over the years, but feel free to pick up a copy of *Digital Image Transfer: Creating Art with Your Photography* (Horovitz, 2011). This full-color book is filled with step-by-step applications of many more methods than would fit in this book and will be a welcome resource for your practice.

Image Transfer Basics

Below are some of the basics (and differences) of what you can do using photocopy machines (ubiquitous at agencies and offices), scanners, inkjet printers, and laser printers. This ought to whet your appetite and get you started. What you can do with a photograph and the aforementioned is only limited by your creativity and your knowledge of specialty substrates.

Photocopy Machines

A photocopy machine is an electronic duplicator that fuses a reproduced image to plain bond paper. This is heat transferred as opposed to a home or office inkjet machine. Photocopy machines are often used for outputting various kinds of papers (Grafix has a heat-transferred paper, and some Lazertran papers require heat transfer for placing your work onto silk substrates, etc. – this will be covered in the section on threaded applications later in this chapter). When transferring with Citra Solv (which I prefer to use as opposed to acetone or Xytol, which are toxic), the substrate can *only* receive the image if it has gone through a heat-based output, such as that which you can obtain from a photocopy machine or a laser printer. In addition, photocopy machines are great for reproducing images by distortion (e.g., wiggling the image over the reproduction glass plate as the light passes) or for outputting onto bond paper for acetone transfer.

Figure 4.1 Here, the original photograph (left) was moved over a photocopy machine and reproduced as a black-and-white output (right). Note how the mother and child image duplicated. This is particularly interesting since this image is of my mother, who was bipolar. These kinds of accidents can lend themselves to discussion in the context of phototherapy.

Example

Figure 4.1 shows an example of using a photocopy machine to distort the image of a photograph. Figure 4.2 shows the final image made using the Linn method over the image to create a translucent effect and then sewn. For more on the Linn method, see Horowitz (2011).

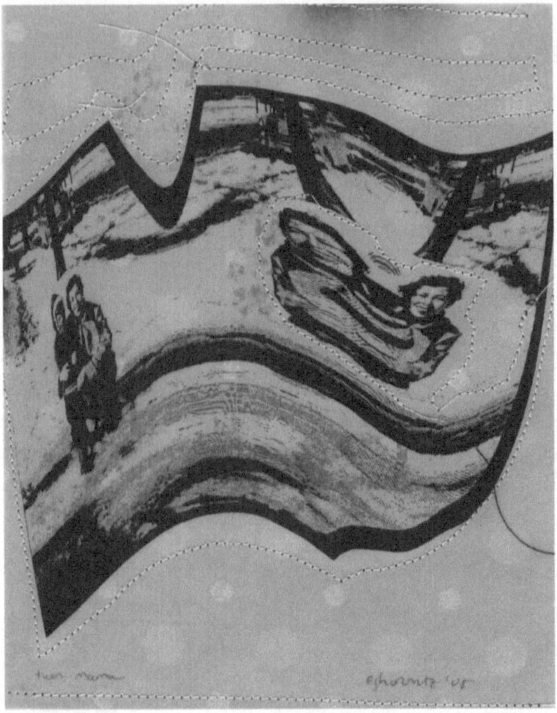

Figure 4.2 The black-and-white image from Figure 4.1 in its final format.

Scanners

A scanner is a device that optically scans an image, printed text, handwriting, or an object, and converts it to a digital image. Even images that have been manipulated through, for example, transferring with acetone, Xylol, or Citra Solv can be further manipulated with any software, then produced onto another surface such as wood, and then scanned back into your computer for further manipulation and/or output. So think of the scanner as your personal digital duplicator and friend.

Scanners are capable of reproducing perfected images of final projects to be further manipulated in future software programs and/or other projects. You can also photograph your projects and then take them back into the computer. If you don't have access to a photocopy machine, you can move your finalized images over a scanner glass and get the same results as by distorting with a photocopy machine.

Example

Figure 4.3 shows an example of taking a photograph created from Polaroid 669 film (left), scanning it back into the computer, and then playing with it in Photoshop, Studio Artist, and Artmatic software to create the finalized image (right).

Figure 4.3 From analog film (left) to digital output (right) using a scanner and software: Photoshop, Studio Artist, and Artmatic.

Inkjet Printers

An inkjet printer uses minute jets of ink to transfer the image to bond (computer) paper or specialty papers. Some papers, such as Sheer Heaven (only available at Cre8it (www.cre8it.com)), are specifically made for inkjet printers and not intended for laser printers. However, certain transfer papers, such as inkjet papers by Grafix and Lazertran, are made to go through these home-based printers. Any deviation may result in unwanted and less effective output.

Example

Figure 4.4 shows an example of using Sheer Heaven paper. After the paper goes through the inkjet printer, it is sprayed with 70% alcohol. Then the paper is rubbed onto the substrate (cardstock in this instance) and the result is on top. (Above is the image transferred onto cardstock; below, I used the byproduct to create another image, since it was too beautiful to discard.)

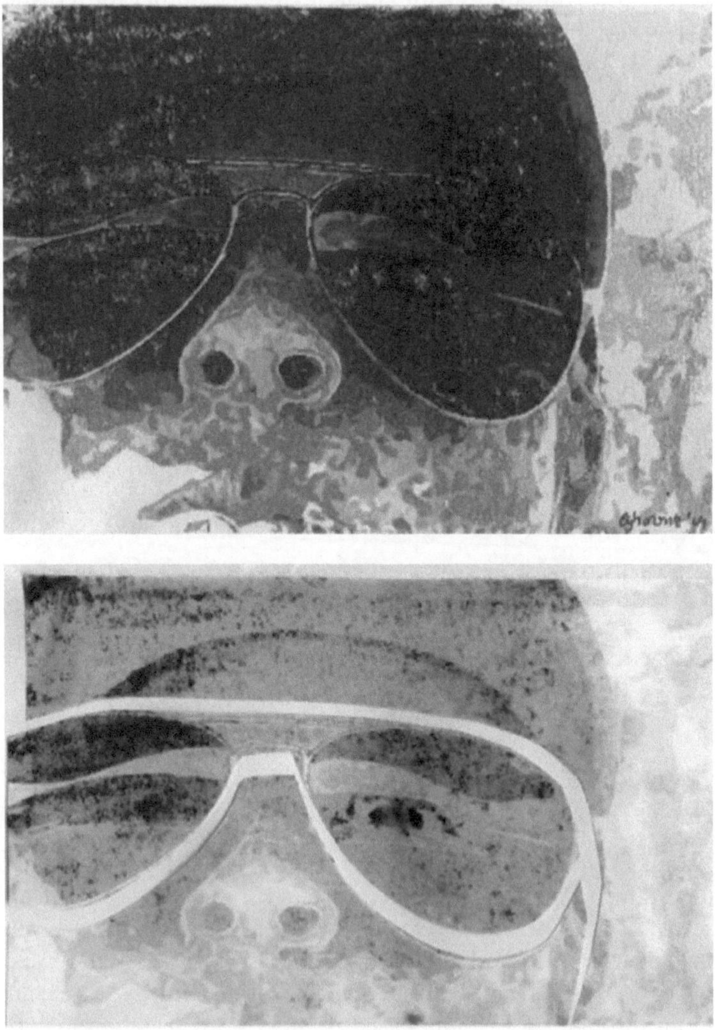

Figure 4.4 Top: Sheer Heaven specialty paper. Bottom: Its byproduct.

In addition, just to offer the reader another example of specialty papers and output with inkjet printers, Figure 4.5 shows an example of Grafix paper printed via an inkjet printer and then adhered to a rock before making permanent with Permalac varnish spray *(N.B.: Use Permalac spray in a well-ventilated area and don a protective mask.)*

Figure 4.5 Grafix specialty paper transferred onto a rock and fixed with Permalac varnish spray.

For more methods using inkjet printers, see Horovitz (2011).

Laser Printers

Laser printers are heat based and are used with a variety of available commercial papers (Lazertran, Grafix, etc.). Dry ink (toner) particles are electrostatically picked up by the drum's charged areas and print the image onto paper by direct contact and heat, which fuses the ink to the paper. You can then use the image and transfer it onto a variety of materials including metal, fabric, polymer clay, and paper.

Example

Figure 4.6 illustrates the work-in-progress pictures with various tools, dies, and Premo Sculpey polymer clay (www.sculpey.com). Figure 4.7 shows a working example of using Lazertran Silk paper, running it through a laser printer, and then transferring it onto Sculpey. *(N.B.: The image should be reversed as it is a mirror image; when it includes writing, this is critical.)* The paper is then burnished (print side down) onto the surface of the Sculpey and left for 30 minutes. Then the Sculpey is placed in a tray of water (for about two minutes); the paper floats off, leaving the image on the Sculpey. Next, allow the Sculpey to dry for an hour. It can then be further manipulated, adorned, and then baked to hardness at 275 degrees Fahrenheit (135 degrees Celsius) for 10 to 20 minutes. For further directions and other methods for using laser printers, see Horovitz (2011).

Figure 4.6 Premo Sculpey polymer clay, tools, and work in progress.

Figure 4.7 Grave plaque for Sophie and Dali, created using Lazertran Silk paper and burnished onto Premo Sculpey polymer clay.

The Case of C

In this next case, C used numerous phototherapy techniques in our three-year span together. While the patient used paints, clay, and traditional media, C also gravitated towards phototherapy techniques in order to make transitional objects for comfort (Winnicott, 1953). Figure 4.8 shows C's genogram, which outlines multiple psychiatric issues and contention with being born a biological female. C liked to be referred to as "he" during our treatment and so that is how I will refer to him from this point. Additionally, C told me that a woman sexually abused him at a playground (when he was 5); however, there was no ability to verify this information with either parent or others. As a result, he was totally fixated on being a male (he took hormones so he could grow a beard, and packed a potato in his underwear to approximate a penis), and fantasized about marrying his attractive residential worker, W.

Because C relived his mother's abandonment (at age 5) despite numerous individual and familial sessions (with both father and mother), much of his work revolved around his grief at the loss of his mother. Figure 4.9 illustrates a sample of his work around this psychological trigger. From a photographic image, C printed onto fabric an image of his mother and himself. (See printing on muslin using a laser printer (Horovitz, 2011, pp. 64–66) and discussed later on in this chapter (freezer paper as a transfer medium).) Sewing the image onto the pillow allowed C to affix this image and later "sleep" with his mother; he also carried the pillow around much like a transitional object as described by Winnicott (1953).

Cyanotypes or Blueprints

During our sessions, C used another phototherapy method: cyanotypes. Blueprints (or cyanotypes) use ferric ammonium citrate and potassium ferricyanide. These days, you can purchase pretreated cloth, watercolor paper, and a variety of other substrates from sources such as Blueprints on Fabric (www.blueprintsonfabric.com). Basically, an object (such as a leaf, a stone, a key, or whatever you fancy) or a negative (or digital invert) is placed on top of the treated surface and exposed to the sun and/or other means of development such as a mercury vapor lamp or UV lighting. When the blueprint is exposed to ultraviolet light, the ferric iron of the citrate is reduced to the ferrous state. After exposing the treated surface to bank light (the sun), a mercury vapor lamp, or UV fluorescent light tubes in the 300- to 360-nanometer range (black lights), the article is simply rinsed with water, which fixes the image permanently. *(Hint: Adding a capful of bleach to the water solution will brighten the blues.)* The result is an insoluble iron salt, ferro ferricyanide, that permanently stains the treated area. Should you want to make your own cyanotype mixture, I have provided the formula in Table 4.1. *(N.B.: Care should be taken to work in a well-ventilated area and to don a protective mask and gloves while both mixing and storing the chemicals in a light-tight container. Caution: If you do mix the chemicals yourself, unused solution should be washed down the drain with copious amounts of water. Dilute with eight times more water than solution and never pour down a storm drain or directly into the ground.)*

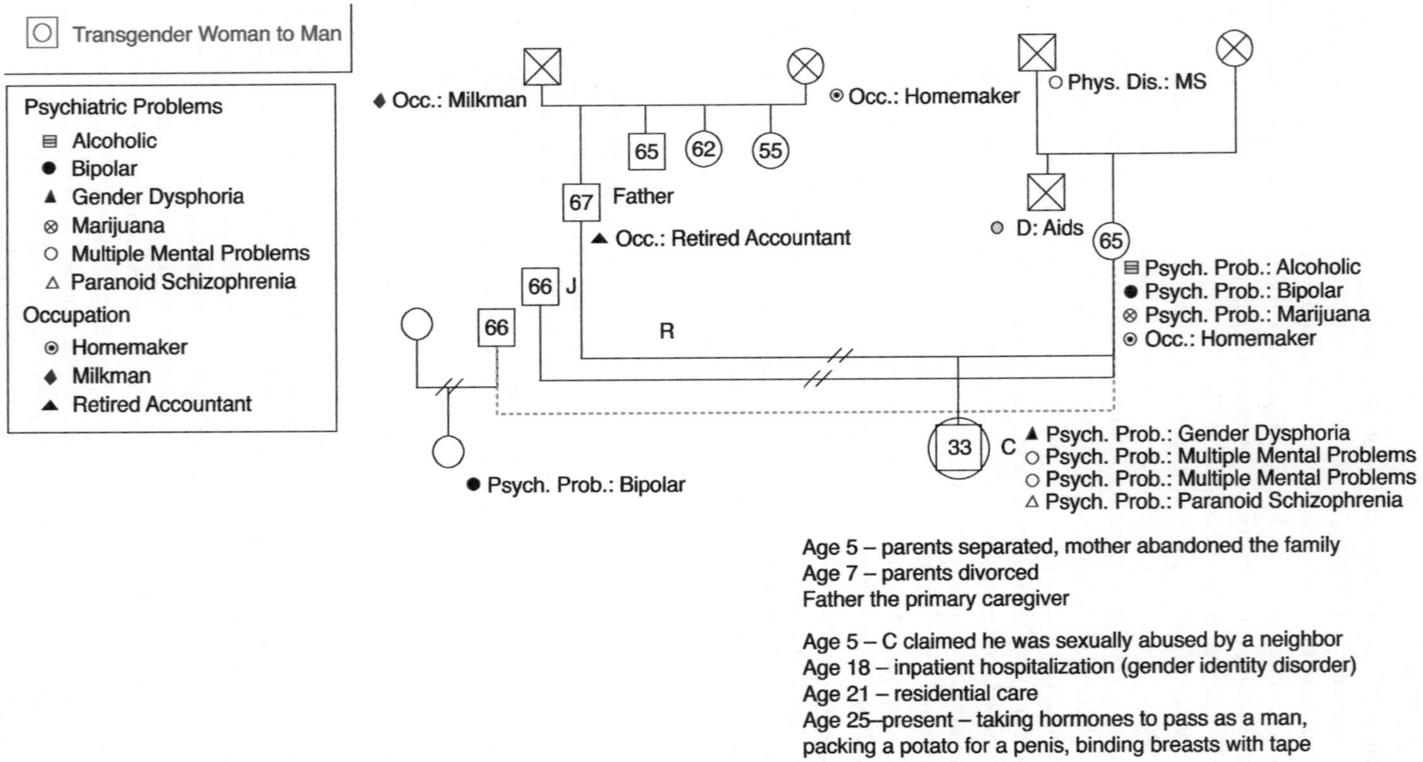

Figure 4.8 C's genogram. (Printed with permission.)

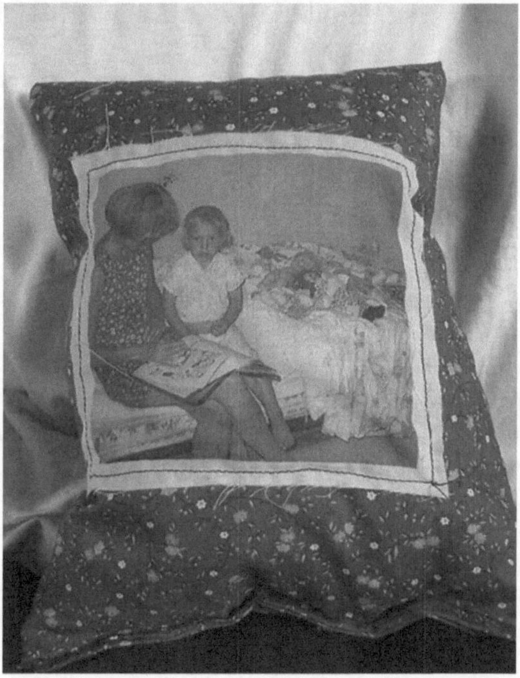

Figure 4.9 C's transitional object, a pillow with an image of himself at age 4 and his mother. (Printed with permission.)

Table 4.1 Formula for creating your own cyanotype mixture.

Water	*Potassium Ferricyanide*	*Ferric Ammonium Citrate*
1.2 gal.	4 oz	8 oz
2 qts	¼ lb	½ lb
4.5 gal.	2 lbs	4 lbs
6.5 gal.	3 lbs	6 lbs

1 gallon will treat 6 yards of fabric

Blueprints only work on natural surface fibers: cotton, silk, linen, and viscose/rayon. You can print on prepared yardage, linens, tote bags, watercolor paper, canvas – well, the possibilities are endless if you prepare the solution yourself. Synthetic fibers will not print. Cotton/polyester blends will print but the result will be less intense. This is because polyester does not react with the blueprint chemical; only the cotton part of the fabric will print. In addition, blended cotton/polyester fabrics will "fade," since the cotton component tends to abrade. Canvas will print because the fibers are tightly woven. Whatever fabric you use, make sure that you prewash and remove sizing and/or conditioners before exposing to the cyan chemical mixture.

While you can do this outside, the ideal temperature is between 65 and 75 degrees Fahrenheit (18–24 degrees Celsius) and when the sun is directly overhead (generally between 10 am and 3 pm). In general, when the temperature is above 80 degrees Fahrenheit (26 degrees Celsius), decrease the exposure time. If the temperature is below 60 degrees Fahrenheit (15 degrees Celsius), increase the exposure time. Recommended general exposure times are as follows:

- hot summer days: 5–10 minutes
- cool, bright spring days: 8–15 minutes
- cold, clear winter days: 15–20 minutes

Heavier fabric needs more exposure time.

To learn how to create your own UV light box, see Horovitz (2011, pp. 127–130). You can also remove the blue and change the color of the outcome; again, to learn more about that, see Horovitz (2011, pp. 132–134).

Figure 4.10 shows an example created by the author where the color has been altered and changed. Figure 4.11 illustrates another example of a transitional object created by C, this time using family images and outputting them as cyanotypes. These blueprints were then sewn onto Barney fabric before being sewn into a pillowcase.

Figure 4.10 A blueprint with some of the cyan removed and then tea-stained and colored (created by the author).

Figure 4.11 C's Barney pillow with family images in cyanotype. (Printed with permission.)

Population Benefits and Contraindications

Printing on fabric using a laser printer or using phototherapy techniques is a wonderful medium for almost any population. As long as you are well versed in how to use digital applications to manipulate photographs (e.g., inverting them (making negatives) and/or flipping the images (mirror imaging)) and other basic techniques involved in using some of these applications, you can easily stretch into digital applications with your patients. Mashable has a list of places where you can learn your way around Photoshop: http://mashable.com/2010/10/08/free-photoshop-tutorials/#.NtWb09NUSqD. Gimp is very comparable to Photoshop and is free: www.gimp.org/downloads.

However, my favorite website for learning just about any software is Atomic Learning (www.atomiclearning.com). At Atomic Learning, you can learn just about anything from Photoshop to Illustrator, InDesign, Final Cut Pro, Flash, etc. The best part is that you can work right alongside the video instructor and, if you own the program that you are learning, you can open up your own document/graphic and work on your project as you learn. It is the next best thing to having a personal instructor, since you can return again and again to the application for a brush-up. As stated at the beginning of this chapter, in this digital age, you owe it to yourself and your present and future patients to be at least as competent as they are. Recently, a patient told me that her 3-year-old went on her iPad without her knowledge and placed several episodes of *Paw Patrol* in her cart. While she was aghast that he had done this, I told her to go home, celebrate just how bright her child was, and place parental controls on *all* of her devices!

Even if your patients are not skilled in digital techniques, here is where your abilities can act as a "third hand," as suggested by Kramer (1986). To quote Cathy Malchiodi (2012b), art therapists can use a

> third hand to enhance a client's creativity without being intrusive, imposing one's own style or artistic values, and misinterpreting meanings found in images. Ultimately, the responses of the therapist to a [client's] process of art making reflects and supports that client's worldview, creative potential, and ability to use art for reparation and recovery.

My advice to the incipient digital artist is practice, practice, practice. Given the fact that I was reared on white-out, typewriters, and the *Encyclopedia Britannica*, we have come a long, long way. My maxim is *carpe diem*. Learning is power.

SolarFast

SolarFast is a permanent and washable sunlight-developed dye that is used to create photographic prints on fabric or paper using a film negative. The company has even made this accessible to those who do not know how to turn an image into a black-and-white photo or negative (invert). The Jacquard SolarFast Negative Generator (www.jacquardsolarfast.com) can be used for turning your photographic images into film negatives for use with SolarFast dyes. To create a film negative, you can upload any image, convert it to black and white, invert it to create a negative, and print it through an inkjet or laser printer onto SolarFast film or another transparent film – basically, acetate made for either inkjet or laser printer output (it is important to make sure that the acetate is rated to go through your specific type of printer). Using SolarFast dyes, you will be able to print any image onto any natural fabric (100% cotton, silk, etc.) or rag paper. Figure 4.12 is a screenshot of an image that was manipulated using the Jacquard SolarFast Negative Generator.

Figure 4.12 A screenshot from the Jacquard SolarFast Negative Generator.

Basic Steps to Creating Your SolarFast Image on Fabric or Paper

1 Keep in mind that your SolarFast print will only be as good as your negative. To achieve truly white highlights on your print, for example, the darkest areas of your negative must be adequately opaque. Hold your negative up to a light source to make sure that it is completely blocking light in its densest areas. Depending on your printer, you may need to print two negatives and sandwich them so the solid black areas are truly opaque. Alternatively, you may want to run the film through the printer a second time or adjust the printer settings to output more ink.

2 For hard edges, use masking tape to create a window the size of your image. Coat the print area evenly and completely but don't soak it. You want the dye to be damp, but not overly wet. Blot the fabric with a rag or paper towel to remove excess dye before exposing. When printing on a t-shirt or garment, place a piece of paper or board between the layers to avoid bleed-through.

3 It is recommended that you apply SolarFast to your fabric under a photographic safelight (or in a very dimly lit area). Place your negative, waterproof acetate side down (print side up), directly on the wet surface. The negative must be flush against the wet painted surface. For best results, place a piece of glass or acrylic over the negative. Alternately, you can hold the negative down with tape, pins, magnets

or clips – just make sure that the negative is pressed flat against the painted surface. Once you have applied SolarFast to your fabric, place your negative (printed on acetate if done digitally) on top. Keep the negative in place and then cover the entire image with black plastic or cardboard before taking out to the sunlight.

4 Next, expose the fabric or substrate to sunlight for 10 to 20 minutes, wash it, and that's it – creating photographs on fabric or paper is that easy! Different colors require different exposure times, ranging from 10 to 24 minutes, depending on the weather conditions and time of day. See the recommended exposure times shown in Figure 4.13. For indoor printing, use a 400-watt black light, such as the Eliminator EBK 400.

5 Wash your print to complete the color development and wash out excess/undeveloped dye. For textiles, machine wash on the hottest setting. Use SolarFast Wash for best results.

6 For paper prints, hand wash by submerging them in the hottest tap water possible, add SolarFast Wash (1–2 capfuls or 10 ml), and keep the water flowing for at least ten minutes. The exposure chart for the 14 different colors that SolarFast offers is shown in Figure 4.13.

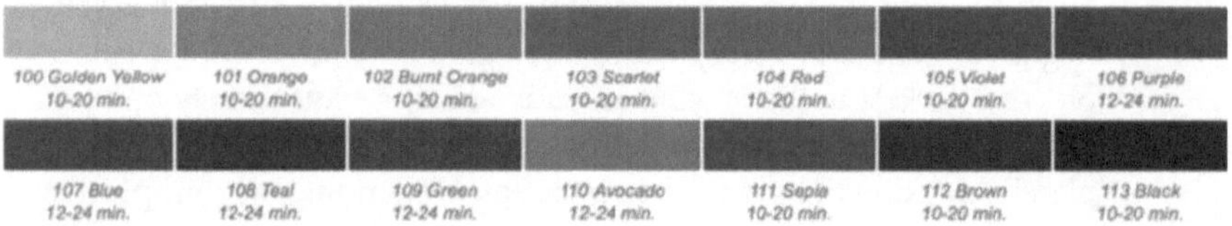

Figure 4.13 Recommended exposure times for SolarFast colors.

For more info, or to see videos of SolarFast, go to: https://vimeo.com/72210081.

SolarFast dyes can also be used to create photograms, shadow prints, and ombrés on fabric and paper, no film required. It can also be used for painting, tie dyeing, screen printing, stamping, batik, and more. For detailed instructions, tips and techniques, FAQs, and troubleshooting, go to www.jacquardproducts.com/solarfast.html. Figure 4.14 shows examples of SolarFast on two cotton t-shirts. SolarFast is a great alternative to cyanotypes since there are 14 colors available to use with patients. The beauty of this product is its simplicity and ease of use. It can be used with any population and can even be used to make something as simple as photograms.

Tips from the SolarFast Site

- You can combine negatives with objects for more diverse effects. Place a ribbon, tools, or leaves over your negative, for example, for combined effects.
- You don't have to use SolarFast only on white fabric. Consider printing on previously dyed fabrics, patterned fabric, your old clothing, or even found paper. The background color just has to be lighter than the SolarFast color you are using. (Dyes are transparent, so the under color will affect the resulting color of the print. Printing yellow on a blue fabric, for instance, will produce a green print.)
- Rather than using a printed negative, you can draw or paint directly onto a transparency and make a print from your hand-painted design. Just make sure that whatever you paint with is opaque (Sharpie permanent markers work great!). Use a paintbrush, paint pen, applicator, airbrush, or silk screen to apply the opaque ink to a transparent film.
- SolarFast does not need to be heat set, steamed or chemically fixed – it just needs to be exposed to sunlight. This makes it ideal for embellishing or repairing artwork on fabric. Use SolarFast to color in a design or to add accents to a piece of artwork. You can also use it on top of another SolarFast print to fill in areas or to superimpose images.
- SolarFast makes the ultimate screen-printing ink: no heat setting required, soft to the touch, no in-screen drying, permanent, and cleans up with water. What's more, you can superimpose images and create continuous tone prints. Screen printing is a great way to apply solid blocks of dye without having to mask off areas or use a brush. Screen printing SolarFast is also a great way to superimpose imagery onto a pattern:

    1 Use SolarFast Thickener to bring the dye to the desired viscosity. Print as normal.
    2 While still wet, expose the print to sunlight.
    3 After exposure, wash in hot water with SolarFast Wash.
    4 To superimpose an image, simply lay a negative on top of the print before exposure, as directed in the SolarFast instructions.

- For SolarFast printing on wood, the wood must be clean, uncoated, and untreated. Use pine or a light-colored wood for best results. Balsa works great and is highly absorbent.

    1 Sand off any finish before applying the dye. After exposing, you will have to hand wash the wood surface.
    2 Use a sponge to gently scrub the surface.
    3 Use hot water and keep it submerged at least ten minutes.

Figure 4.14 Examples of SolarFast on t-shirts created by the author.

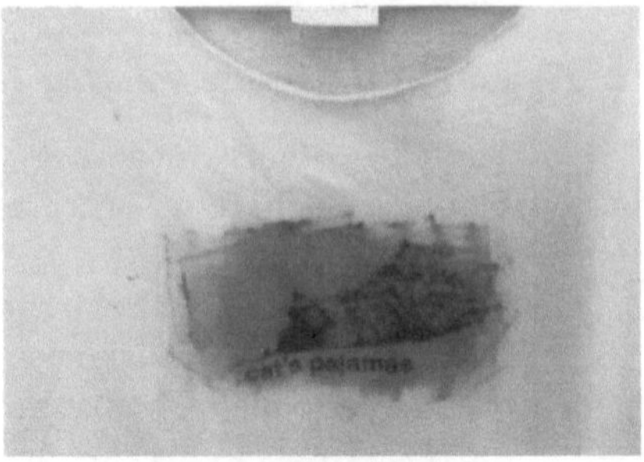

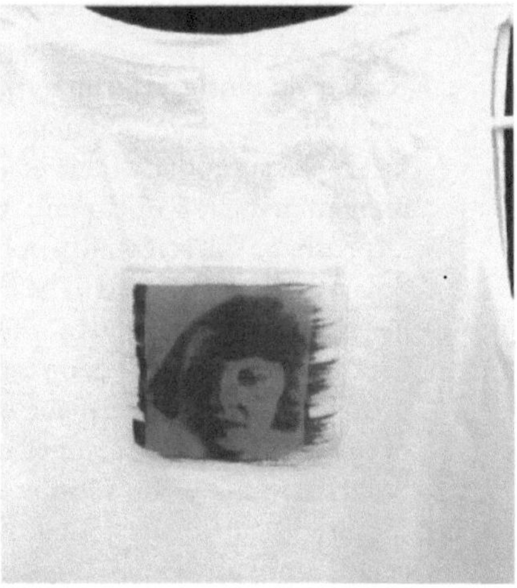

Population Benefits and Contraindications

SolarFast is a wonderful medium for self-expression and can be used by any population, on the condition that the art therapist is comfortable with the medium and either has access to outdoor space in which to work with patients or to somewhere where the SolarFast dye can be exposed to a 400-watt black light, such as the Eliminator EBK 400 or similar. In addition, it is best that the fabric be prepared ahead of seeing your patients, placed in a black plastic bag (or light-tight photographic box), and ready to go. While it is recommended that the material be slightly damp prior to placing the invert atop, I have found that the results are the same if the fabric is dry. While you can do this in real time with your patients, access to a safelight is *vital* so that the SolarFast dye will not be exposed before placing the invert (or photogram) on the treated fabric. Using SolarFast dye to create wearable artwork can truly raise self-esteem, bolster ego maturation, and function as a transitional object between sessions similar to working with cyanotypes.

Premo Sculpey

While this section scratches the surface of polymer clay and liquid clay and its history, I encourage the reader to peruse Horovitz (2011), Mitchell and Mitchell (2003), and Pavelka (2002) in order to delve more deeply into the properties and endless possibilities of this wonderful art medium. In this section, the basics of this art form will be covered so that you can get started in this amazing transfer medium. While there are numerous manufacturers, for the examples in this section, I used Premo Sculpey (the strongest of the polymer clays, while soft enough to be easily conditioned) as well as Liquid Sculpey (either as a binding agent or by itself).

Conditioning

No matter the brand, all polymer clays need conditioning for maximum pliability. Furthermore, conditioning evenly restores the PVC molecules. This can be easily done right from the package by kneading the clay with your hands and an acrylic brayer, but the optimum method is to run it through a modified pasta machine (Figure 4.15).

Filtration of the Clay

The polymer clay exudes an oily residue and sometimes people (who exude lots of body heat from their hands) find it difficult. To leach the clay, you can extrude it through the largest pasta setting and then place the clay between several sheets of freezer paper; the oily stain that appears on the paper the next day leaves the clay with a more manageable consistency.

Coloring and Tinting

Beyond using pigments to embed into the translucent quality of the medium, you can add in paint or other powder-based pigments (Mica, Jacquard Pearl Ex, etc.) to alter the color of the Liquid Sculpey, antique it by applying and removing pigment, and even stipple it over another medium such as papier-mâché, should that be your aim. Should you want to use specific colors, it is possible to make your own hue other than through sheer transfer.

Baking

Larger projects can be baked in a conventional oven. While the manufacturers say that it is safe to resume baking in these ovens once Sculpey has been processed, we recommend that you designate an old toaster oven specifically for smaller projects. (You can readily find these at thrift stores or garage sales.) In addition, *always* preheat your oven for at least ten minutes before baking your projects; if not, an undesirable burnt cast to the medium can appear. The temperature baking range generally operates between 260 and 275 degrees

Fahrenheit (127–135 degrees Celsius); for every ¼″ (6mm) thickness, bake for 15 to 20 minutes. (Some art therapists choose to do the baking of the artworks post-session, but this is entirely up to you as well as your comfort level with the toaster oven.) *(Caution: If the clay is burning, you will notice a toxic fume. While the clay naturally casts off an odor when baking, if a pungent odor persists or smoke alarm goes off, turn off the oven, leave the room, and ventilate the area.)*

Transferring Images onto Sculpey

You can transfer images directly onto Sculpey using a laser printer to print out your image in black and white (rotated in mirror image). Use regular computer (bond) paper. You can add color later by coloring the black-and-white images with Prismacolor pencils before burnishing onto the clay. While numerous polymer clay artists recommend gently spraying the image with water to impregnate the image onto the clay, I recommend the following technique (Figure 4.15):

- After conditioning the clay with an acrylic brayer or a converted pasta machine, lay the image face down and burnish.
- Let the clay sit with the image for ten minutes. Then lightly burnish again with 70% alcohol until you can see the back of the image on the back.

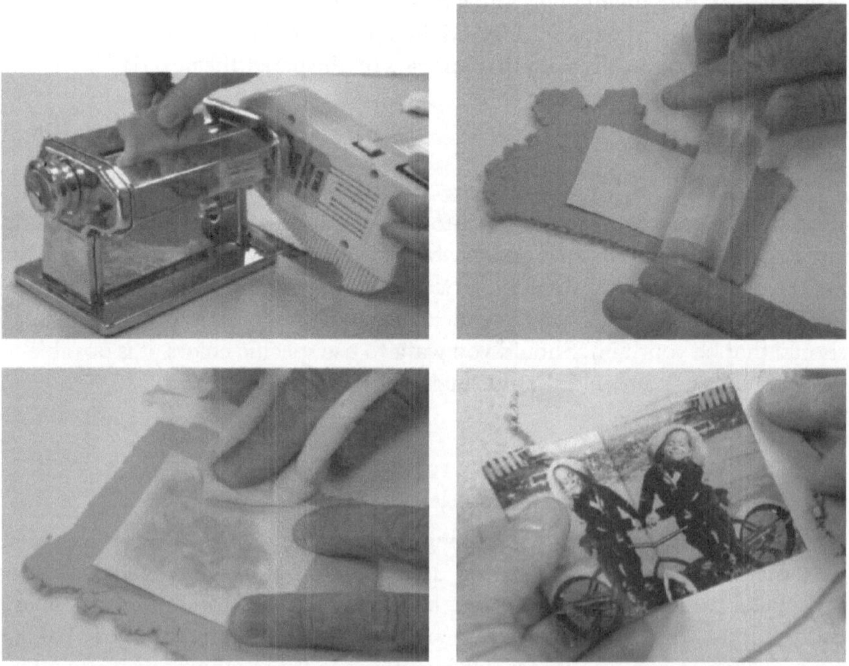

Figure 4.15 Steps for transferring a laser photographic image onto Sculpey.

- Let the image rest for three to five minutes; place on freezer paper and put it back in the toaster oven for two minutes before peeling off the paper. Then complete your baking process.

(Hint: If stored properly, polymer clay can be kept for many years. (It does tend to become stiffer over time and if it will not condition, it is entirely possible that the clay has partially cured and is unusable.) Polymer clay can start hardening at 80 degrees Fahrenheit (7 degrees Celsius), so be careful not to leave it in your car's interior on a warm summer day. Also, always start working with the lightest-colored clays first so that the residue on your hands does not rub off onto lighter colors handled later. Cleaning your hands with a baby wipe between colors used eliminates some of the problem.)

Case Study: Using Sculpey with Burn Survivors

Sculpey can be used by itself to create artwork, as illustrated in Figure 4.16. The images showcase artwork created by burn survivors in a group. The images on the left show part of an island project created with Sculpey, and a close-up of a tiger, fashioned by an adolescent male (approximately age 18), who was horribly burned over 85% of his body; he also had a tracheotomy tube so that he could speak. The tiger became a subject that repeatedly appeared whether he was working in paint, papier-mâché, or, as in this case, Sculpey.

The artwork shown in the right-hand image of Figure 4.16 was created using a matchbox as the form for the final box. This artwork (aptly named "Boxy" by

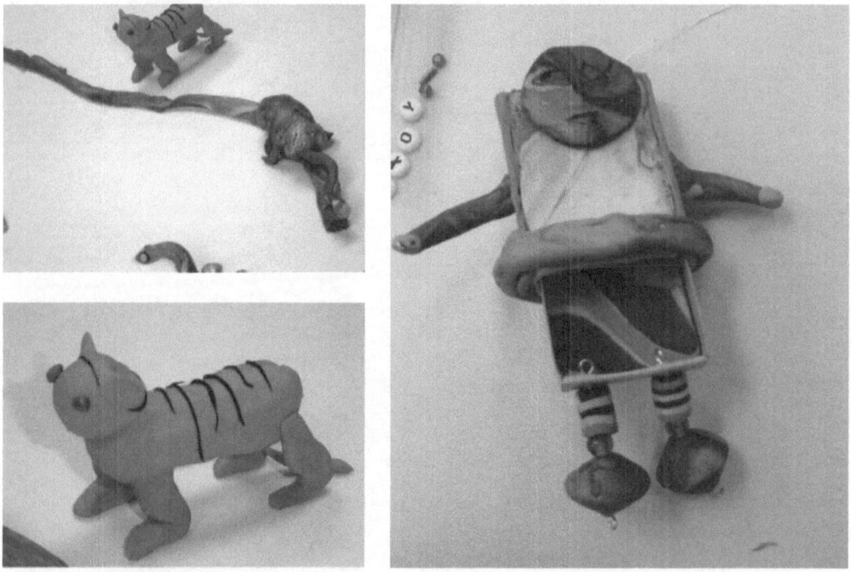

Figure 4.16 Artwork created by the Burn Survivor Adolescent Group. (Printed with permission.)

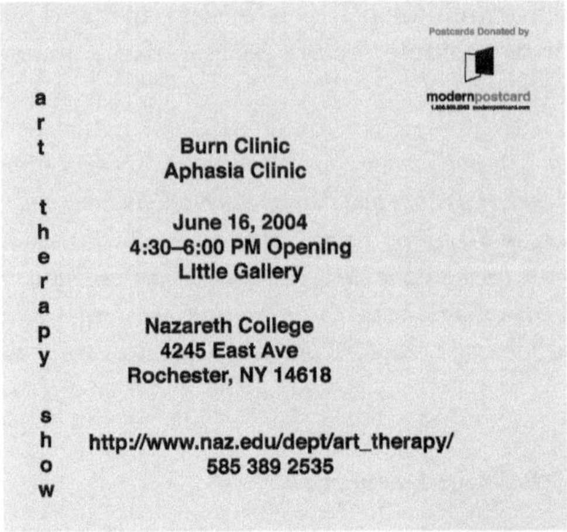

Figure 4.17 Top left: A postcard advertising the opening of an exhibition of the Burn Survivor Adolescent Group's artwork. Top right: The reverse of the postcard: an image of the Sculpey figurine "Boxy" that was also used for the cover of a book (Horovitz, 2005). Bottom right: Business cards to sell Sculpey earrings. (Printed with permission.)

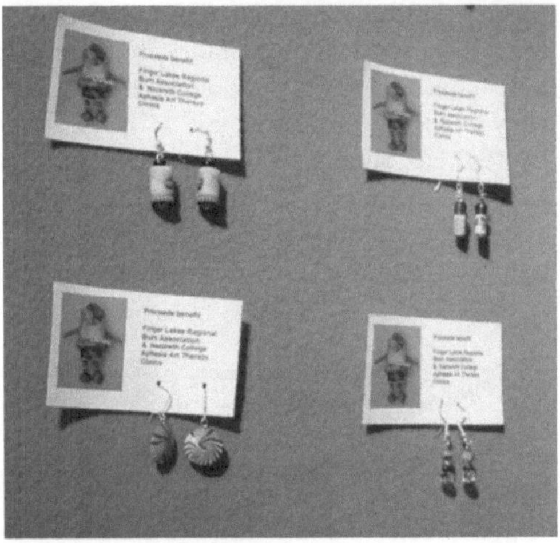

Figure 4.18 A Sculpey pin created by a 59-year-old female stroke survivor. (Printed with permission.)

the 12-year-old female patient) was a source of great pride for this burn survivor as it was used to announce the opening of an exhibition of the artwork, on business cards to sell the Sculpey earrings that were made to support the group's activities, and on the cover of the author's book, *Art Therapy as Witness: A Sacred Guide* (Horovitz, 2005) (Figure 4.17).

Population Benefits and Contraindications

Polymer clay is a wonderful medium that can be used without a conventional kiln, should the art therapist not have one available. Unlike clay, it comes in a host of colors, and, using several techniques discussed in Horovitz (2011), can be striated, patterned, and colored with Jacquard Pearl Ex powder pigments. Images can be readily transferred onto the medium by using specialty papers such as Lazertran Silk (Figures 4.6 and 4.7) or bond paper printed through a laser printer (Figure 4.15) and the techniques that I have outlined here. Because of its ease of use, pliability, and non-messy qualities, it can be used for three-dimensional work when patients resist media such as clay or plaster, which are often messy and dusty, and can lead to regressive responses. Therefore, if you have a patient who might be more on the obsessive-compulsive spectrum, polymer clay is a wonderful medium for self-expression. Polymer clay has proven to be a terrific material when used by populations of all ages and therefore its use does not seem to be restricted to any particular age group. In fact, because of its ease of use and pliable nature, it is particularly effective as a medium for stroke survivors who may have compromised fine and gross motor coordination (Figure 4.18).

Clear Packaging Tape

To transfer an image onto packaging tape, use a laser printer to print your image. A heat-based toner machine (laser printer or photocopy machine) produces the best result. The method is simple enough: just follow the steps described below and illustrated in Figure 4.19.

Transferring Images onto Clear Packaging Tape

1 Using Photoshop or a similar software program, print your image onto your substrate (cheap bond paper works fine). You need not reverse your image. If you print in black and white, you can add color or make marks with colored pencils. The Prismacolor brand works particularly well. Carefully cut out the image printed from the laser printer or photocopy machine.
2 Place your image directly under the clear packaging tape with tacky side touching the actual toner-based image. You can use 3M Scotch packaging tape or a similar product. Uline (www.uline.com) makes the widest non-commercial tape available (6″). *(Hint: Uline tape is difficult to manipulate, so it helps to have a partner to hold one end while you cut the end piece. Together, press the substrate carefully to the tape. It is easiest to tape the substrate and the tape directly onto a table. While you can lay strips of clear packaging tape side by side to make a larger image, you can do this with a partner, as it is very difficult to line it up perfectly by yourself.)*
3 Tape directly to a smooth surface with the printed image under the tape.
4 Burnish the image using a Lineco Bone Folder and Scorer, the back of a pair of scissors, a piece of wood, or the back of a spoon. The important thing is to burnish the entire image to the tape. When doing this directly onto the top of the tape, you can actually see what you are burnishing (or missing if so desired).
5 Soak the tape in a tray of water and very gingerly remove the back of the paper until the resulting paper dissipates, leaving only the image on the tape itself. A small elephant-ear sponge seems to work well, or carefully remove the paper by using your finger. Above all, patience results in the best transfer and eliminates the possibility of tearing the tape.
6 Transfer the taped image onto any workable substrate, decorative paper, or even fabric.

As shown in Figure 4.19, the image is transferred directly to muslin. If desired, you can add a little glue (such as Mod Podge) between the tape transfer and the fabric to make certain that the bond is complete. If there seems to be any air between the tape transfer and the fabric, the Mod Podge serves to insure that the result is cemented to the underlying fabric. These finished products (such as those shown in Figure 4.19) make great homemade postcards, one-of-a-kind cards, or altered art when fully embellished.

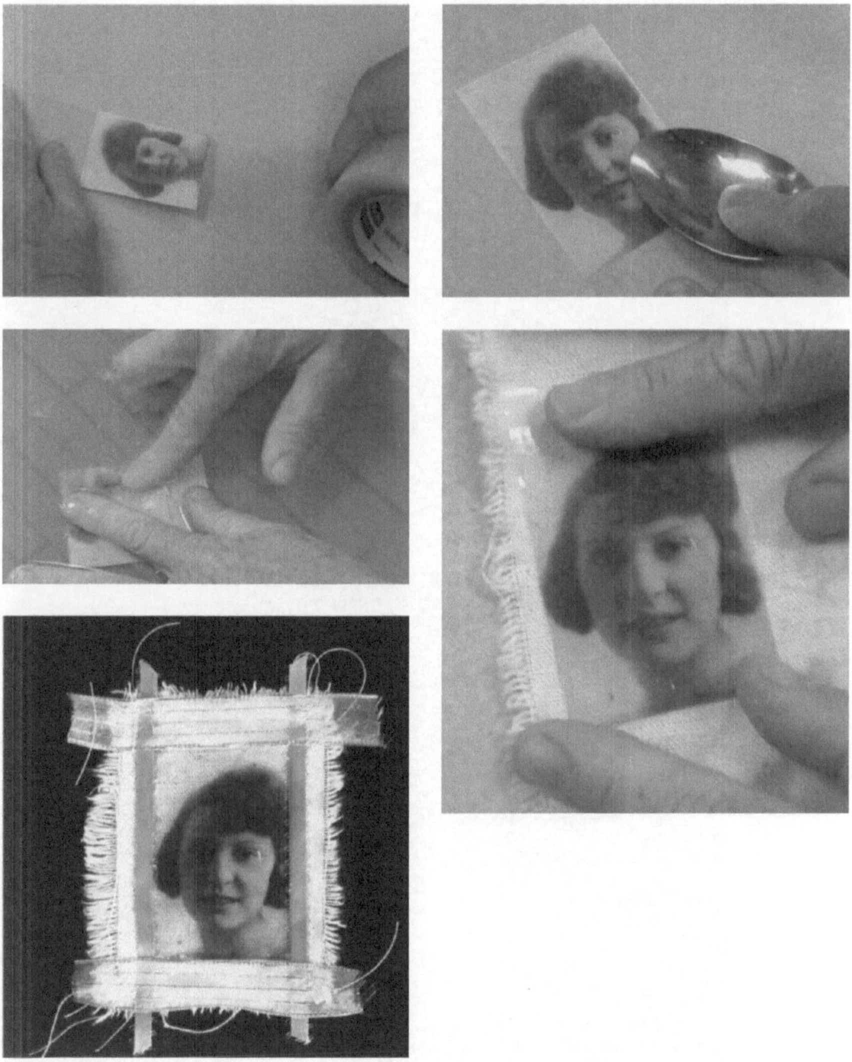

Figure 4.19 Transferring an image onto clear packaging tape and then directly to muslin.

Case Study: Using Clear Packaging Tape to Create a Self-Portrait

For the artwork shown in Figure 4.20, the directive for the patient was to create a self-portrait using this tape transfer technique. Magazine images were scanned, printed, and then cut out for the facial area. The facial images were transferred using the clear packaging tape method and then placed directly onto cardstock. Small holes were cut out for the patient's eyes. Then she adorned her body with old clothing and found objects both from the studio and the environment. Using

Figure 4.20 "Blessed Mother," a patient's self-portrait; mask created using the clear packaging tape method.

this method in her sessions allowed for the unusual exploration of issues, and in this instance, spiritual and cultural issues came to the forefront through this phototherapeutic enactment. The patient was the photo-director in this situation (Horovitz, 2016b; Weiser, 1993). Her idea to be photographed standing in front of a green-board (similar to the blackboards of yesteryear) allowed for further exploration about being schooled Catholic and the effects that this had on her current psychosocial struggles with both religiosity and authority figures.

Population Benefits and Contraindications

Using clear packaging tape is a wonderful means of transferring any type of image, be it photographic or graphic, as seen in Figures 4.19 and 4.20. Because of the ease of using clear packaging tape as a transfer medium, it can be used with any age population, allowing for the therapist to work directly with the patient, since working with the tape is best handled by more than one individual. Furthermore, if working in a group dynamic, this method also works well and instills cooperation between the formed dyads. Contraindications might occur when removing the paper from the packaging tape, as some patients might be averse to keeping their hands in water. In addition, the paper must be removed gingerly in order to avoid tearing the tape. Therefore, patience is required in order for a successful outcome. For patients who struggle with frustration tolerance, this might be a great way to instill fortitude, tolerance, and persistence.

Freezer Paper

Freezer paper is a wonderful medium that can be cut to the size of printer paper (8″ × 11″) and then ironed onto fabric such as muslin, cotton, or lightweight canvas. While you can use either an inkjet or a laser (heat-based) printer to do

Figure 4.21 A ghost byproduct on freezer paper.

this, permanent results only occur with a laser (heat-based) printer or a photocopy machine. It is best to feed in the fabric/freezer paper one page at a time. It is also advisable to cut any loose threads so that it goes smoothly over the printer rollers and exits without any mishap. You can reuse the freezer paper about ten times, and an interesting effect is that each time it goes through the printer with another image, the ghost of that image transfers onto the freezer paper. You can use the freezer paper (with multiple images) as a byproduct for another project. Figure 4.21 shows an example of the "ghost" on a freezer paper that has gone through the printer multiple times.

Transferring Images onto Fabric Using Freezer Paper

1 Precut your fabric to 8″ × 11″ using computer paper as a template. (I also use the computer paper to precut my freezer paper.)
2 Use an iron to attach the freezer paper to the fabric. Use a low to medium heat setting. This seems to works well with most fabric, but you may need to experiment. Be certain to use a pressing cloth or release paper between the iron and the fabric, so that the freezer paper (if exposed) won't stick to the iron by mistake.
3 Place the ironed fabric/freezer paper into your printer, making sure that the fabric is the right side up to receive your ink. (Check your printer as to whether the fabric/freezer paper needs to be fed in with the fabric side facing up or down. This depends on your printer. If you open the paper drawer, it will be clear from the illustration which way the fabric side should face. If you are still unsure, place a large X on a piece of bond (computer) paper and run a test through your printer. If the ink appears on the side marked X, you will be certain which way to load the fabric/freezer paper.)

(N.B.: While commercial fabric paper can readily be purchased to go through your printer, the cost of using the freezer paper method is pennies as opposed to what you might spend on specialty papers available on the open market.)

The output of the fabric/freezer paper method can be used for a multitude of projects. Figure 4.22 shows three different creations of pocket tissue holders. The holder in the top image was sewn using cyanotype fabric discussed earlier in this chapter; the holders in the middle and bottom images were created using freezer paper and muslin fabric run through a laser printer. Creating a pocket tissue holder is a very easy project that can be done using a sewing machine or created by hand.

Figure 4.22 Top: A pocket tissue holder created using a cyanotype. Middle and bottom: Pocket tissue holders created using the freezer paper and muslin fabric transfer method.

Several sites are available to help to make these tissue holders, including YouTube videos. However, the basic instructions are below.

Instructions for Making Pocket Tissue Holders

1 To start, cut a rectangle that measures 5½″ × 6½″ from the fabric that you have chosen for the *outside* of your tissue cover *(N.B.: This will also be the measurement for the image that you might want to print onto your fabric. Bear in mind that you will be cutting this image in half when separating the opening.)* Then, cut a second rectangle of fabric measuring 5½″ × 7½″ if you want to line the fabric. (This fabric is also seen on the edges of the opening, so it's nice to choose a fabric that co-ordinates well with your cover fabric.) *(N.B.: I did not do this for the pocket tissue holders shown in Figure 4.22 so as not to disrupt the image. Instead, I cut the back image the same size as the front: 5½″ × 6½″.)*
2 Place the two pieces of fabric right side together, and sew a ¼″ seam down both the 5½″ sides. If you have decided to line the fabric (using the 5½″ × 7½″ piece), it will be larger than the outside over-fabric, and the piece that you have sewn won't sit flat. That's fine! It means you're doing it right! Turn the fabric piece right side out and press, so that you have approximately ¼″ of the lining fabric showing at the sides.
3 Fold the edges towards the center (you should be looking at the lining fabric). Stitch a seam along both short ends. Then turn your cover inside out.
4 Take the plastic wrapper off your travel tissues and slip them inside your beautiful new fabric cover. Ta da – you now have a personalized pocket tissue holder!

Population Benefits and Contraindications

The cyanotype shown in the top image in Figure 4.22 is an image of my sister and I when younger. I take it with me everywhere; it gives me great comfort to keep my sister "in my pocket" for times when I need a little consolation. Using images of loved ones can be reassuring in times of mourning or quiet desperation. We *all* have ups and downs and having such a calming image so readily available (whether in your pocket or handbag) can uplift the corners of your mouth when life just seems to pull you down. My private patients (adult population) have made pocket tissue holders for themselves and for their children. One patient placed images

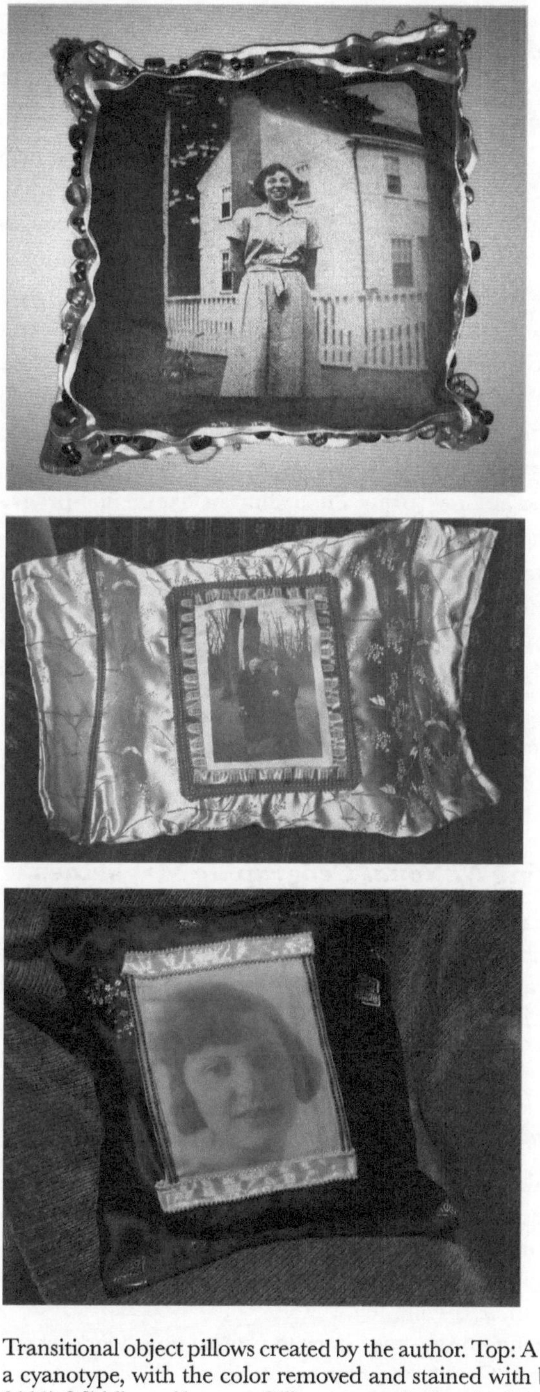

Figure 4.23 Transitional object pillows created by the author. Top: A pillow created using a cyanotype, with the color removed and stained with black tea (Horovitz, 2011). Middle and bottom: Pillows created using the freezer paper and fabric transfer method.

of the *Sesame Street* characters Grover and Elmo on the front of her pocket tissue holder. On the back was an image of her holding her child. Her child gets to keep Grover and Elmo in his pocket as well as his mother, when she is not near. This serves as a transitional object when he is in preschool. Printing onto fabric can be turned into pillows (Figure 4.23 and Figure 4.9, C's pillow discussed earlier), wearable clothing, bags, tote bags, pocket tissue holders (Figure 4.22), or whatever your imagination suggests. You can also manipulate photos with software and get unusual results. The only contraindication for using this technique is connected to whether or not you (1) have access to a laser (heat-based) printer (although an inkjet printer can be used, even though less permanent), (2) are comfortable with either hand or machine sewing (should your patient want to make bags, pillows, pocket tissue holders, tote bags, clothing, toys, etc.), and (3) have minimal graphic abilities (using Photoshop or like digital programs). (If you are not comfortable with digital applications, again, the basics are covered in Horovitz, 2011.) Providing that the art therapist is willing to lend a third hand both in computer/printer output and/or sewing techniques, this can be a marvelous medium to use with any population. Printing on fabric can be an excellent choice when working with populations who experience low frustration tolerance, as the outcome is immediate, tangible, and permanent.

Citra Solv: Using *National Geographic* Magazines

Because of a special coating used for printing the *National Geographic* magazine, Citra Solv, when liberally applied to its pages, dissolves the inks, and often creates unusual abstract designs. *(N.B.: Magazines should not be older than 12 years or the ink may not work.)*

Supplies Needed

- Spray bottle (This is optional as you can sprinkle or use a brush to apply the solvent.)
- Sponge brush or chip brush (Either of these will work.)
- Glass or hard plastic container. (Do *not* use Styrofoam to place the Citra Solv in, as it will melt.)
- Plastic sheeting or garbage bags to protect your working surface
- Paper towels, Q-tips, and cotton swabs

- Citra Solv concentrated formula (either Valencia Orange or Lavender Bergamot)
- Cosmetic wedge sponge (These are available at dollar stores, drug and beauty supply stores.)
- #3 round watercolor brush
- Derwent Inktense water-soluble pencil (I like these pencils because once they are wet, they become like ink and are permanent. You can use other brands of watercolor pencils.)
- Mechanical pencil
- Craft knife (X-Acto)
- Tissues
- Heavy drawing paper, cardstock, or a file folder to create your stencils
- *National Geographic* magazines less than 12 years old (You can often find *National Geographic* magazines at thrift shops, yard sales, and on eBay. Libraries may sell you their back copies for a very reasonable price. I subscribe to this magazine and have for years so the benefits of doing so are twofold: (1) the magazine is educational and (2) the pages can later be repurposed for artistic endeavors.)

The Process

I find Citra Solv's natural citrus and lavender scent pleasant to work with, but since you will be using so much of the product, the fumes can be very strong and may be offensive to others. You may want to work outside or in a well-ventilated area. The covers and advertising on the first and last pages of *National Geographic* are not printed the same as the rest of the content in the magazine, so, before you begin, remove them and any inserts. Do not forget to open the foldout pages. You can also tear off part of the foldout and insert it somewhere else in the magazine. Some artists like to remove the pages that are mostly black ink because they can create a mess. However, sometimes black ink creates most of the textures, so do not be surprised if some of the more colorful images without black ink do not work as well. You will learn as you go which pages work best for you. *(N.B.: There are copyright issues using any of the images, so it would be wise to make sure that they are not recognizable. When I dissolve my magazine, by the time I have finished manipulating the inks and using stencils, the original photographic image is unrecognizable.)* You can spray Citra Solv on the pages, making sure that you have good coverage, or paint it on with a sponge brush or soft brush. You can also drip it from the bottle by holding your finger over the opening.

Allow the Citra Solv pages to sit flat for at least 15 minutes. To speed up the process, you can weight the pages (Figure 4.25). Start checking the pages to see if the ink has done its job. I wait an hour and weight books atop bubble wrap or plastic wrap placed on the Citra Solv pages. (Pressing a piece of plastic wrap or bubble wrap on the page while it is still very wet yields beautiful results.)

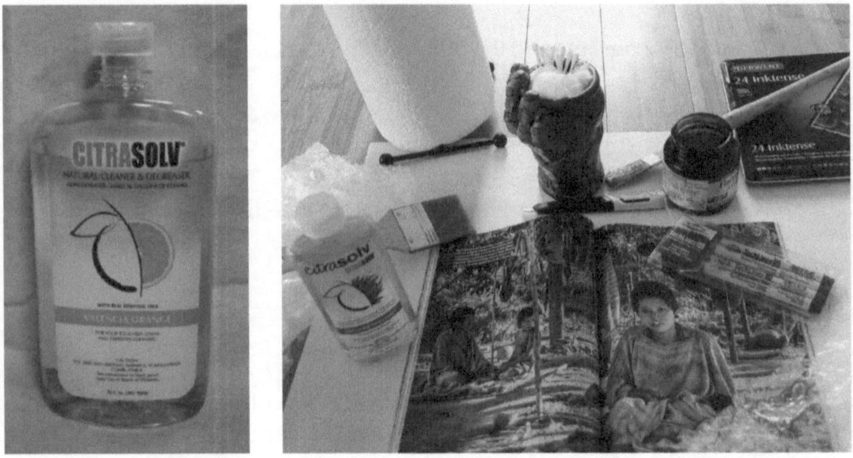

Figure 4.24 Left: Citra Solv product. Right: A *National Geographic* magazine surrounded by various items for manipulating the images.

When I see something I truly like, I remove the weighted books from the page and begin the rest of the process of using inks and stencils to further manipulate the image. While stencils are available on the open market, I like to make my own using cardstock and a mechanical knife to cut out the image. Note that the negative and positive of the stencil can be used (Figure 4.25).

How you open the magazine and pull back the pages also affects the texture. By lifting slowly a little at a time, you can create interesting layers and vertical designs. Quickly pulling the page up, almost a snap from the top or bottom, creates another look. Try different ways to open the pages and manipulate the ink. You can also place a piece of paper or another treated page on top of a very wet page and lift to a monoprint texture. Figure 4.26 illustrates the method of painting the pages with Citra Solv, opening the pages after ten minutes to stop the CitraSolv from dissolving further, and then the final image after manipulation with both positive and negative stencils, Derwent Inktense Pencils, etc.

Another method of working with the *National Geographic* images is to tear out the pages with a technical knife (an X-Acto knife), coat the pages with Citra Solv, and lay either bubble wrap or plastic wrap atop the pages. Next, you weight the pages with heavy books and periodically check how the image is dissolving before manipulating further with stencils, etc. Figure 4.25 illustrates this process of working with bubble wrap and plastic wrap to dissolve the image. (And frankly, I can't think of a better use for the *DSM-5*!) Figure 4.27 shows another example of using these finalized images further. In this instance, the paper has been adhered to tissue boxes and then coated with Mod Podge or Permalac so that the final product is both attractive and durable.

You can even go a step further by taking a digital image of your final piece (Figure 4.28) and then printing it out on muslin so that you can quilt the image

Figure 4.25 Top left: A *National Geographic* magazine coated with Citra Solv and covered with bubble wrap (left) and with plastic wrap (right). Top center: The magazine weighted with books. Top right: Removing the plastic wrap to check the reveal. Bottom left: Using stencils to remove more Citra Solv. Bottom right: The final images produced with bubble wrap and stencils (left) and with plastic wrap and stencils (right).

Figure 4.26 Top: A *National Geographic* magazine painted with Citra Solv. Middle: The revealed image after the pages have been closed for ten minutes. Bottom: The final image after manipulation with positive and negative stencils and pencils.

Figure 4.27 Tissue boxes made with *National Geographic* magazines dissolved with Citra Solv.

to your liking. Figure 4.29 shows my finished image, titled "Birdhouse." This quilted image, my first, took hundreds of hours to finish with thread painting and trapunto techniques. These techniques will be covered in the section on threaded applications.

Figure 4.28 A Citra Solv *National Geographic* magazine image manipulated with bubble wrap and stencils.

Figure 4.29 "Birdhouse" (18″ × 24″), a quilted image finished with thread painting and trapunto techniques.

Using Laser Printers and Citra Solv

This process is quite similar to the one for using Citra Solv with *National Geographic* magazine images. However, in this instance your substrate for the Citra Solv transfer can be cardstock or muslin (Figures 4.30 and 4.31) or metal or wood (Figure 4.32). In order to use Citra Solv to transfer onto fabric, wood, or metal surfaces, you must first digitize and reverse the image, especially if words are involved. It's a good idea to follow the steps below.

Transferring Images Using Citra Solv and a Laser Printer

1 Be sure to tape or pin your copy from a laser printer securely to the receiving surface and the work surface.
2 Use a piece of cotton, a cosmetic sponge, or a brush to apply the Citra Solv.
3 Do not use too much Citra Solv; use just enough to see the image appear on the back of the paper. You can add more after the first rubbing.
4 Use a bone folder or a spoon on a hard surface to transfer the image with a firm even pressure. If you use a spoon, use the bottom, working in circles. You can also turn it on its side for tight details.

(Hint: If you are using Citra Solv on fabric, burnish the image onto the fabric, then wait a few minutes, and then iron the image into the cloth to penetrate the fibers. Wait 24 hours before hand or machine washing the finished article.)

Figure 4.30 Top left and top right: Transferring Citra Solv and an image to cardstock. Middle left: Citra Solv-soaked paper pinned to muslin. Middle right: Rubbing the Citra Solv-soaked paper onto the muslin with a spoon. Bottom left: Ironing the burnished Citra Solv image into the muslin. Bottom right: The finished product.

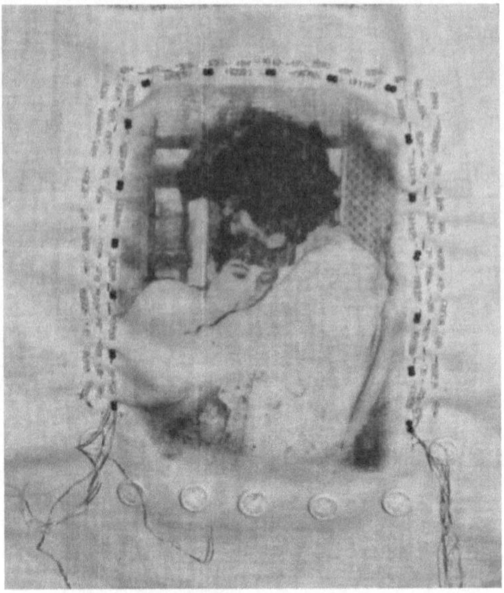

Figure 4.31 An example of Citra Solv and an image transferred onto muslin and adorned with old buttons and beads.

The metal surface shown in the left-hand image of Figure 4.32 was first roughed up with extra fine steel wool (#000) for this transfer. Because the metal surface is nonabsorbent, you need to use very little Citra Solv. Add a little more where needed only after the initial burnishing with a spoon and check regularly. Use this same method when transferring onto a wood surface but be a bit more liberal with the Citra Solv as the wood tends to absorb the solvent.

Figure 4.32 Left: Citra Solv and an image transferred onto metal and then sprayed with Permalac so the image permanently remains. Right: Citra Solv and an image transferred onto wood and sprayed with Permalac.

Figure 4.33 An example of a *National Geographic* magazine processed with Citra Solv, created by an adult contending with mourning and loss issues. (Printed with permission.)

Population Benefits and Contraindications

As can be seen, Citra Solv is a very economical and versatile product for use with preadolescents through to adults. It is a marvelous product for making collages (Figures 4.25–4.32). Because of its immediate process when working with substrates such as tissue paper, cardstock, and fabric, it is a terrific product to use with patients who have little patience and are extremely impulsive. Nonetheless, care needs to be taken when using the *National Geographic* magazine process as it takes time for the Citra Solv to penetrate the magazine inks. For those patients who are challenged with impulse control issues, using Citra Solv on *National Geographic* magazines, metal, and/or wood requires tempering impulsivity and waiting for the process to yield the reveal. This may be demanding at best. Therefore, the art therapist needs to plan accordingly. On the other hand, if your objective is to increase frustration tolerance while building self-esteem, Citra Solv is an excellent medium of choice. Because of its inherent ease of use, it can be used with patients challenged by cognitive, neurogenic, or physiological constraints.

Photofusing onto Glass

Fusing photographs onto glass can create a keepsake to treasure for years to come. The process is fairly simple and can be used with almost any photograph, though black-and-white photographs are recommended for this project due to the absence of certain chemicals found in color photos. The first step is to de-saturate the photos on your computer using image-processing software (Photoshop or the like). In addition, you need to pay careful attention to the printer that you are using since the toner specifications for the ink cartridges differ from printer to printer. However, to print on Delphi Glass Decal photo paper, the toner specifications for your printer need to be high in iron oxide to withstand the temperature of the kiln once the glass fuses to the glass-fusing photo paper.

This very interesting technique of using glass photo paper, a laser printer, and kiln to create images that are permanently fused onto glass has numerous applications. The necessary supplies and steps to create such artworks are listed below.

Photofusing Images onto Glass

Supplies Needed

- Fusing photo paper for a laser printer (I use the glass photo paper from Delphi (www.delphiglass.com)
- Black-and-white laser printer that uses toner with high iron oxide content (most HP models will work)
- Digital photo manipulating program (i.e., Photoshop) to turn color photos to black and white and resize (useful for putting many pictures onto one 8.5″ × 11″ sheet so as to not waste the transfer paper)
- Distilled water
- Shallow tray for the water
- Small squeegee (optional)
- Fusible sheet glass COE 96 (I use clear, but color is acceptable – it depends on preference)
- Scissors
- Various colors of glass frit, various colored glass stringers, etc. (these are optional, but if used must all be COE 96)
- Glass cutter
- Running pliers
- Ruler
- Sharpie permanent marker
- Paper towels
- Kiln: Paragon Janus multi-purpose kiln with a Sentry 2.0 controller (kiln schedules will vary depending on the type of kiln used)

- Ceramic fiber paper or shelves that have been properly cleaned with kiln wash (to prevent glass from fusing to the kiln shelf) (fiber paper can also be used to create a channel in the glass during the firing process for threading purposes if it is intended to hang the finished product).

Method

1 Prepare the digital files: convert color photos to black and white and resize as necessary (300 dpi works well) to fit on an 8.5″ × 11″ sheet.
2 Warm up the printer by printing five blank sheets before you place the fusing photo paper into the laser printer for copying.
3 After removing the tissue paper coating, load the transfer paper into the printer. Be aware of the orientation necessary to load the paper correctly for your printer model and print on the coated shiny side of the paper.
4 Print your sheet(s).
5 Cut out the images (right to the edge of the photo).
6 Map out the quantity and specific sizes needed for your images on the sheet glass using the Sharpie and the ruler.
7 Cut the sheet glass into pieces using the glass cutter, the ruler, and the running pliers.
8 Wash the glass (alcohol works best to get fingerprints and Sharpie off).
9 Fill the tray with distilled water.
10 Soak the images in distilled water, face down, for approximately 30 seconds (a little longer will not hurt). You will know they are ready by gently sliding the paper between your fingers. The decal will lift off the backing paper.
11 Carefully slide the decal off the paper and onto the glass (printed side up).
12 Smooth out any bubbles using your fingers or a squeegee. Gentle manipulation is necessary to avoid tearing and ruining your piece.
13 Blot with a paper towel.
14 Optional: Apply additional colored frit or stringers as desired *(Hint: Apply an additional layer of clear sheet glass to the top, capping the image; this gives the best visual results. Another option is to place a clear glass sheet between two images; doing this will create depth.)*
15 Allow to dry completely (overnight preferably) before firing. Prepare the kiln and load the glass pieces onto ceramic fiber paper or shelves that have been properly cleaned with kiln wash.
16 Fire to 1350 degrees Fahrenheit; the images turn a sepia tone once fired. For complete instructions, see your particular glass-firing kiln.

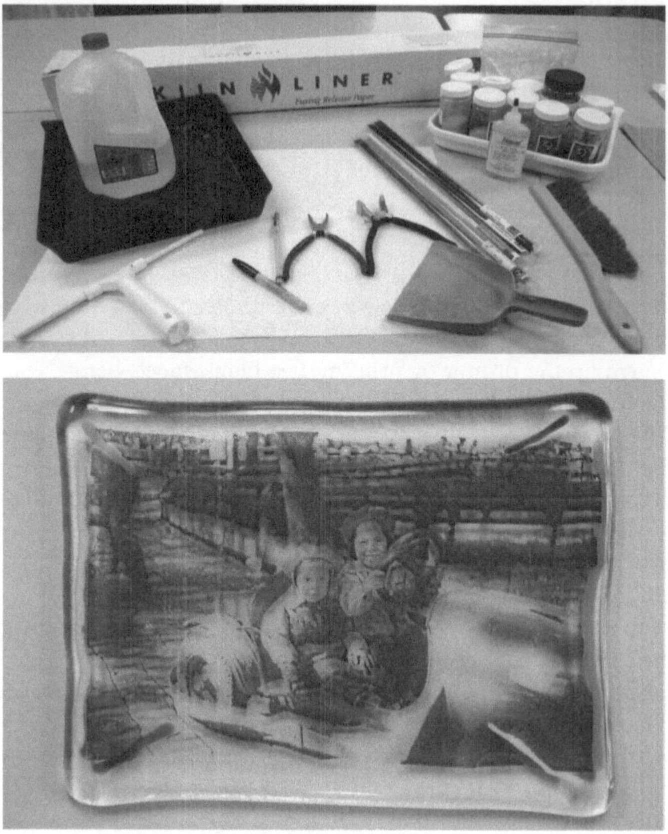

Figure 4.34 Top: Supplies needed for photofusing onto glass. Bottom: A kiln-fired piece.

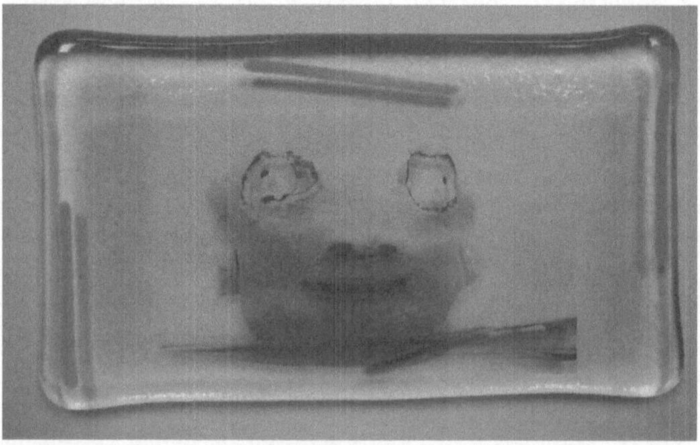

Figure 4.35 An image in glass created by a 9-year-old patient from his clay sculpture. (Printed with permission.)

For more information on all of these steps and more examples of work, see Horovitz (2011). Figure 4.34 shows the necessary supplies and a completed image on glass completed by the author from an image of her sister and brother. A 9-year-old patient created the glass piece illustrated in Figure 4.35. Highly invested in his clay sculpture, he created a photographic image of it, which was then transferred onto glass as a gift for his mother.

Creating in Glass Using Dichroic, Frit, Glassline, and Other Elements

Glass can be used in a variety of ways to create decorative products such as plates, jewelry, pocket vases, etc. The first step is making sure that whatever COE (Coefficient of Expansion) is used, all other elements (frit, stringers, dichroic accents, etc.) are all the same COE. All glass products featured in this book were created with COE 96. Glass is extremely brittle and sharp so the art therapist needs to be prepared for working with such materials. While one might use this particular medium with children and adolescents, personally I think it is better suited to the adult population. Because of the inherent danger of being cut, one needs to be mindful, have a first aid kit at the ready (should accidents occur), and always proceed with caution. In most instances, if a patient is uneasy around the glass-cutting materials, I create all of the necessary cuts (thus acting as a third hand). But once the glass is cut, it is fairly easy to embellish with frit or stringers or by painting with Glassline. Figure 4.36 shows an example of a photographic transfer necklace created with Delphi photo paper and Glassline for embellishments. Figure 4.37 illustrates how the Glassline looks on the glass before firing (left) and how the finished product looks after going through a second firing, using a slump mold (right). I tend to offer these products to my adult patient population. Having an artistic bent is always a boon and more often than not, my private patients fall into this realm.

Figure 4.36 A necklace created by an adult with Glassline and Delphi photo paper. (Printed with permission.)

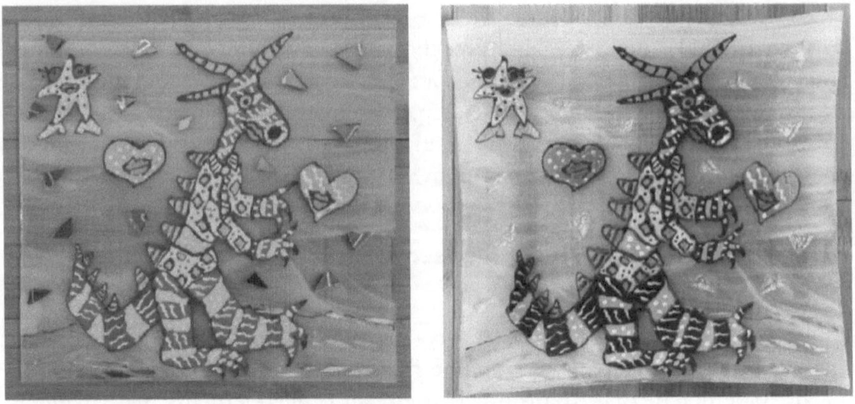

Figure 4.37 An example of a 6″ × 6″ plate created by the author. Left: The pre-fired plate, created using Glassline and dichroic elements. Right: The finished plate fused and then slumped. (Note how the dichroic elements fused into the glass below.)

Finally, you can use glass with other media; Figure 4.38 shows a quilt created by the author. The top image shows the pre-fired glass painted with Glassline and embellished with dichroic elements. The bottom image shows my final quilt as it was assembled; the fabric dinosaurs were created with Pébéo paints on muslin and then thread-painted and embellished with fabric and, later, beads. (Pébéo paints will be covered in the next section, on threaded applications.) The fired glass piece was attached to the upper area of the quilt. This was part of a lapidary quilt challenge. The theme for the challenge was "Treasure."

I called the final piece "The Interspecies Proposal." It measured 20″ × 22″. This quilt incorporated traditional and modern quilting, kiln-fired glass, and hand beading. My title reflected the fact that the kneeling Ankylosaurus male is giving the Allosaurus female a citrine engagement ring while a Stegosaurus male witnesses the event.

Population Benefits and Contraindications

As illustrated herein, glass can be used with Delphi photo paper and a laser printer with at least 30% iron oxide in the printer inks to fuse permanent sepia-toned photographic images onto the fired glass. In addition, glass can be used as a stand-alone medium to create wearable and usable glass art. Using other elements such as frit, stringers, dichroic glass, Glassline, etc. can enhance the final product. As stated earlier, the art therapist should proceed with caution when using this particular medium and know his/her population and limitations. Clearly, the art therapist could be instrumental as a third hand in helping to create the finalized art

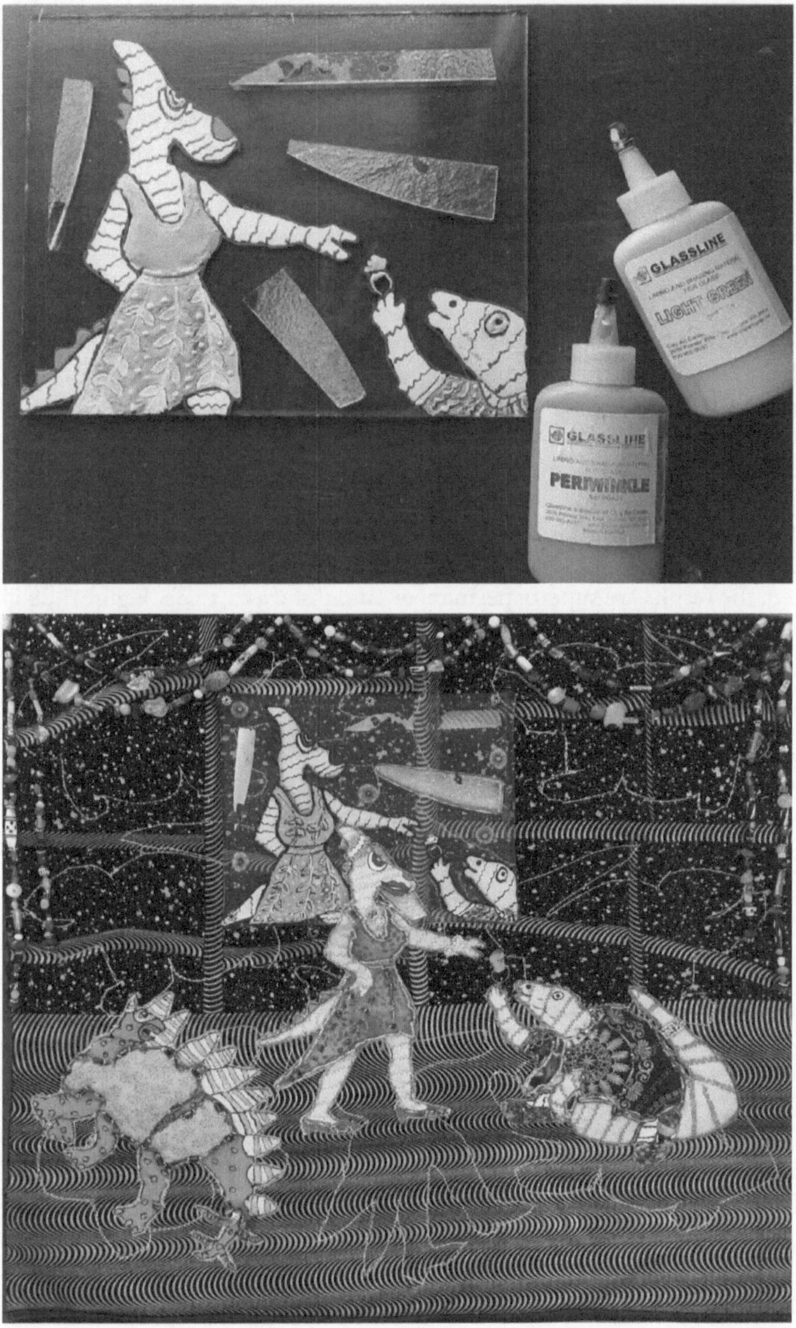

Figure 4.38 Top: Glass painted with Glassline and embellished with dichroic elements, unfired. Bottom: The finished product, "The Interspecies Proposal": fired glass piece and Pébéo painted muslin artwork on a quilt with beaded elements. Artwork by the author.

products. When using glass with patients, the end products can be both beautiful and satisfying. Indeed, with specific populations, it can lead to enhanced self-esteem and self-worth. In addition, handcrafted wearable artworks (such as the necklace) can be transitional objects and can cause attachment issues to surface.

Painting on Existing Glass Products

If you do not have access to a glass-firing kiln, despair not. There are some very advanced products on the market that are in marker form, and liquid paint that can be used on existing glassware and fired in a conventional domestic oven. I have even used Sharpie markers in the past with a variety of patients. I recently stumbled upon the Pébéo line of markers and porcelain and vitrea glass paints. Admittedly, the Pébéo brand is far superior to the Sharpie marker system or, in fact, any product that I have used. The results can be stunningly professional and when the glass is baked and cured in a domestic oven, the results are superb, permanent, and dishwasher safe. Figure 4.39 illustrates the Pébéo Vitrea glassware paints and Pébéo Porcelaine tubes, as well as examples of glassware and ceramic mugs that I created on dollar-store goblets and available glazed mugs. Even though the Pébéo Porcelaine tubes are supposed to be used solely with ceramic or porcelain products, they work equally well with glassware; in fact, the Porcelaine paints allow for the creation of a three-dimensional surface on either glass or ceramic. Directions for firing both products, whether on glassware or ceramic objects, are fairly interchangeable. I do hold the temperature longer than instructed: at least 40 minutes, whether it is for glass or ceramic baking. There are 26 transparent, 10 opaque, and 10 colored tubes available for the Pébéo Vitrea paints. For the Porcelaine paints, there are 46 colors, 18 marker colors, and 12 cloisonné tube paints. The line is remarkable and while the amount might not look like much in the 45ml bottles, the amount required for making the products illustrated in Figure 4.39 hardly made a dent in the paint.

Baking Instructions for Pébéo Vitrea 160 Paints and Porcelaine 150 Paints

Pébéo Vitrea 160 Paints: The items will be tack-free in a few minutes but fully dry after a minimum of 24 hours. Then, bake at 40 minutes at 325 degrees Fahrenheit (160 degrees Celsius) (steady temperature) in a domestic oven, after drying for a minimum of 24 hours.

Pébéo Porcelaine 150 Paints: Bake for 35 minutes at 300 degrees Fahrenheit (150 degrees Celsius) in a domestic oven, after drying for a minimum of

24 hours. For the markers, allow to air dry for 72 hours for decorative use with light washing and no soaking.

(N.B.: I generally bake both items at 325 degrees Fahrenheit (160 degrees Celsius) (steady temperature), making sure to place the items in before turning on the oven. In addition, especially with glass, I allow the oven to cool down to room temperature before moving the objects.)

Figure 4.39 Top left: Pébéo Vitrea glassware paints. Top right: Pébéo Porcelaine tubes. Bottom left: Glassware products created by the author using Pébéo Vitrea glassware paints. Bottom right: Ceramic mugs created by the author using Pébéo Porcelaine tubes and paint.

Figure 4.40 shows two products created by a 35-year-old woman whom I had been seeing in private practice for a variety of issues including post-partum depression, anxiety, physical issues, and PTSD. The first is an oil decanter, made from recycled wine bottles and painted with Pébéo oil paint markers. The second is a candleholder, adorned with rainbows and airplanes, for her dining-table. Both objects depict her main focus for wellness, cartoon characters and symbols

Figure 4.40 Glass artwork created using Pébéo oil paint markers by a 35-year-old woman with post-partum depression, anxiety, physical issues, and PTSD. Top: An oil decanter decorated with cartoon characters. Bottom: A candleholder decorated with rainbows and airplanes. (Printed with permission.)

that her children hold sacred. Since she spends so much time preparing meals for her family, these objects are continual reminders to march towards wellness for her small toddlers, her husband and, most of all, herself.

Population Benefits and Contraindications

As seen in Figure 4.40, painting on existing glass products is an excellent medium that can produce terrific results for patients. While there might be a number of glass-painting products out there, I strongly recommend the Pébéo line since the results are very professional. Furthermore, it can be fired in a domestic oven and so there is no need for a kiln should the art therapist not have access to one. Moreover, the glass is dishwasher safe (upper rack) and when using the paint on ceramic, the same is true. In addition, the paint is microwave safe. In the past, one could only get that kind of reliability with kiln-fired, glazed work. The only contraindications are that you need to factor in drying time of 24 hours before curing in your domestic oven. For those with poor impulse control (who need immediate gratification), this might not be the medium of choice. But for those who can wait, it is an excellent medium far superior to the Sharpie oil marker line, and is a boon for building self-esteem in your patients. Furthermore, this can be used with any age and the Pébéo line even has paint markers if you prefer to avoid using the paint. Thus, it may be more portable for the art therapist on the go.

Threaded Applications and Healing

A Little History

Using fiber in therapeutic arts has been a staple for various cultures, both ancient and contemporary. Healing objects have had a wide range of applications from traditional garb (headdresses, Native American blankets and healing necklaces, etc.) to more contemporary work coming from women's sewing circles and professional artists. Johnson and Wilson (2005) determined that textile handcrafting gave women a sense of place and connected them to their personal histories while providing tangible and intangible benefits.

According to Collier (2011a, 2011b), Feen-Calligan et al. (2009), Hinz (2016), Huss (2010), Moxley et al. (2011), and Reynolds (1999, 2000, 2002), the fiber arts have focused on the healing nature of using these art materials to amplify meditation, communication, and cognitive and analytical skills. Indeed, the use of fiber arts has been claimed to enhance relaxation, soothe fears, distract from intrusive thoughts, build self-esteem, strengthen perceived control and social support, and transform illness experiences (Reynolds, 1999, 2000, 2002). Collier

(2011a) reported that the spontaneous use among women of textile arts such as knitting and weaving decreases negative mood, distracts, and rejuvenates. In Collier's book (2011b), her goal was to formalize the integration of textiles into clinical practice. She made frequent reference to art therapy throughout her book and coined the term "textile art therapy." She noted that although art therapy "typically encourages women to express and vent negative feelings though their artwork," the use of textiles in art making simultaneously encourages women to use their art as "a way to bring about positive mood, relaxation, pleasure, and rejuvenation" (p. 15).

While the use of fiber arts has been reported by Collier (2011a, 2011b) and Huss (2010) to augment meditative, communicative, and analytic/problem-solving skills, Florida fiber artist, Lynne Vantriglia, also utilized fiber arts in women's prisons. In 1994, she began Art Behind Bars, a nonprofit, art-based community service program at the Monroe County Detention Center in Key West, Florida; she collaborated with officials there and conducted two-hour fiber art sessions for inmates (Winebrenner, 2004).

Fiber Arts and Art Therapy

I found Collier's article (2011a) on the well-being of women who create with textiles to be particularly poignant and well researched. She summarized the frequency and pattern of their handcrafting, the reasons for creating with fibers, and whether or not this in fact changed their mood. Collier (2011a) stated, "In both my practice and in my work as a fiber artist, I have found that many women already use their textile handcraft for psychological reasons" (p. 105). She went on to say:

> During my own decades as a textile handcrafter, I have seen firsthand how women use textiles to cope with life, from the joy at the process of making to the joy of giving to someone else . . . . When choosing art as an intervention for psychological exploration, there are obviously a multitude of media to choose from. The results of this study make a case for assessing a client's mastery with textile handcrafts, and for using this medium as a launching point for therapeutic art intervention.
>
> (2011a, p. 112)

I agree with Collier's statement and, in fact, have worked with fibers (threaded applications) since 1975 with a variety of populations including stroke survivors, the blind, and school-aged children. Figure 4.41 shows two off-loom weaving instruments, as well as a quilt of hand-made paper (middle) and a wall hanging (bottom), both made by stroke survivors. Figure 4.42 shows examples of woven art (including woven paper) by school-aged children aged 7–11. Figure 4.43 shows a blind adult making a hat on a cardboard loom that I constructed for him. Knots on the hat helped him know where the color changed.

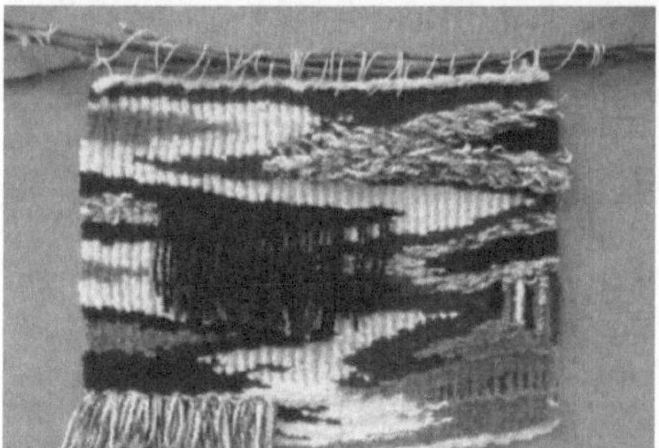

Figure 4.41 Top: Hand-made looms. Middle: A hand-made paper quilt created by a stroke survivor. Bottom: Off-loom weaving created by a stroke survivor. (Printed with permission.)

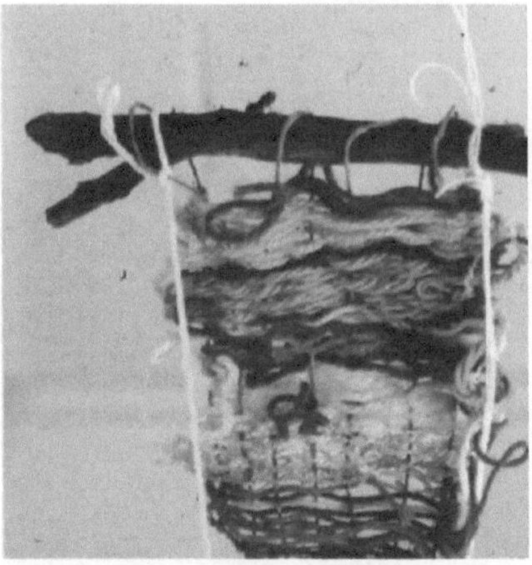

Figure 4.42 Woven products (including paper) created by school children aged 7–11. (Printed with permission.)

While researching this book, I joined several fiber and knitting groups both to educate myself and to meet other fiber artists. I continually experienced that these mirrored the sewing circles that women participated in during times past. The circles often took on therapeutic roles where women talked, shared (and sometimes cried) about personal issues, and sublimated their feelings through their artwork. This was not unlike any art therapy group that I facilitated. It soon became a gathering for embracing new, healthy relationships at a time when I was mourning my own work relationships and friendships that had been deleterious to my soul. It was an added benefit to learn so much (artistically) from these women, and to simultaneously make healthy choices and friends in the process. Because of that, the rest of the work discussed will

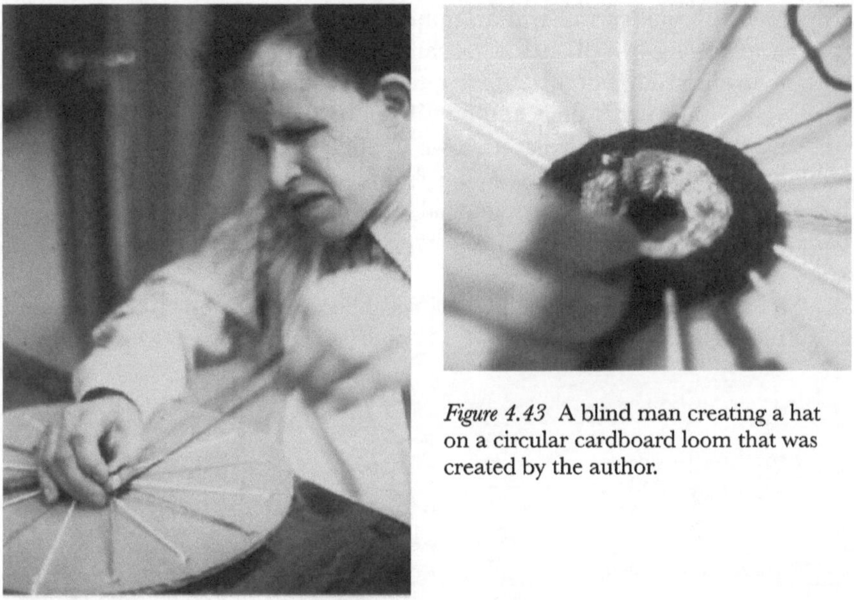

Figure 4.43 A blind man creating a hat on a circular cardboard loom that was created by the author.

center on this yearlong activity that has now become a major staple in my life.

Quilting: The Fiberista Group

Remember playing Telephone Line when you were little? If not, I will remind you how the game worked. Sitting in a circle, you would whisper something into someone's ear. Next, that person would whisper what you said to the next person and so on and so on until the last person whispered back into your ear. Then you would reveal what the last person said. Generally, by the time that last whisper got around to you, the message that you delivered had completely changed. Well, imagine doing that with 12 women in quilt format. So here is how it works: the first person (you) creates a quilt limited only by the dimensions of 8.5″ × 11″. Next, you place your quilt in a 9″ × 12″ envelope and write a page in a small book that will only be seen by the next person who receives your box. (In that box are 11 other 9″ × 12″ envelopes.) The second person removes your quilt and the pages that you wrote. Inspired by your work, she creates another 8.5″ × 11″ quilt, writes what she did in the small book, and places a small file clip on her page so that the third person cannot see what you wrote. She seals your work in a 9″ × 12″ envelope. The third person only sees the second person's quilt and her written entry. And so it continues for 12 months. On the last month (Month 12), all 12 quilts are revealed. In sum, there are 144 quilts since there are 12 women in the group. And what is interesting to see is how your first quilt influenced 11 other women and how you were influenced by other women in the process.

Not being a quilter, this was an uphill challenge for me as I learned how to quilt (throwing myself in a boot camp to do so). I will offer you an idea of how inspired I was by the first quilt box that I received, Mary's quilt. I will show you Mary's quilt and how I responded (bear in mind, the quilts will have long been revealed and shown in public by the time that this book is published). Figure 4.44 illustrates Mary's quilt (which I received) and my quilt response, which warped into a journal, complete with a pencil (with shaved bark). What I wrote to a friend below explains how I cooked this up:

> So I am in this group called Fiberistas. There are 12 women. Each month I receive someone else's 8.5″ × 11″ quilt. The first image, Mary's (giraffe

Figure 4.44 Top left: The front side of Mary's quilt. Top right: The back side of Mary's quilt. Bottom left: The author's closed quilted journal. Bottom right: The inside of the author's quilted journal, including a hand-shaved pencil and scroll tucked into the inner pocket. (Printed with permission.)

> and fabulous boxed quilting to left) was what I received. The elephant was the fabric on the back. Because I had little fabric and being a bit out-of-the-box, I started using Photoshop and gathered images off the internet (including the Swahili writing) and made my own fabric by printing the images on muslin using both the smaller and larger giraffe images and elephants. But then, thinking about Mary's desire to use more African-themed fabrics, and wandering into that journey, I decided to create a quilt/journal, complete with pencil (shaved to look more authentic and of African design) and finally tucked a tiny paper scroll (of the repeated small giraffe images) into the larger giraffe pocket.
>
> Next it will go to Sue, but she won't see Mary's. And on and on to each of the 12 women and all will be revealed in a year from now; and there will be 12 other quilt lines (including the one I started) influenced by each member for a total of 144 quilts! What fun in the name of art for art's sake!!!

Each month, the members of the Fiberistas get together and share new techniques with each other and work alongside each other for about six hours. We share other art projects that we are working on, especially if there is a quilt challenge (such as was the case with the quilt shown in Figure 4.38, which was for the lapidary challenge), and we may offer each other structural ideas to implement and/or just admire the final output of whatever we bring to the group to share. Getting to know 11 other supportive and wonderful artists has been a true gift, my primary gain. Of course, learning new skills was a secondary gain since I was able to pass on what I learned to my patients in art therapy sessions.

And speaking of therapy, I will share one more fiber story. Kathi Everett, an astounding artist who was part of the Fiberista group, was going through a horrendous struggle during the time that her son was deployed in Afghanistan. For every day that he was gone, she created an X square, sewing it onto a quilt (Figure 4.45). The organza Xs had a muted image of the photograph of her son (top left) imprinted on the fabric. The bottom image is a close-up of one of the Xs and when she expected his return. Hand sewing this quilt on a daily basis served to steady her during this frightful time as she anxiously awaited his safe return home. (Thankfully, her son returned from this tour safe and unharmed.) Kathi wrote:

> The moment my son informed me he was to deploy to Afghanistan, my maternal dread was days so his return home would be a tangible reality. With a date stamp, an X stamp, dye ink, and 2″ canvas squares, I diligently and deliberately stamped each passing day. It was important to me to see the blank canvas squares pile get shorter. After reading his journal, I marked, with a black circle, the days he had been in imminent danger. The photo of him at work is printed on organza. Every step of this quilt had its reasons and rewards.
>
> Relying on this daily creative ritual was therapeutic and, in the end, a memorable narrative for my son.
>
> (Everett, 2016)

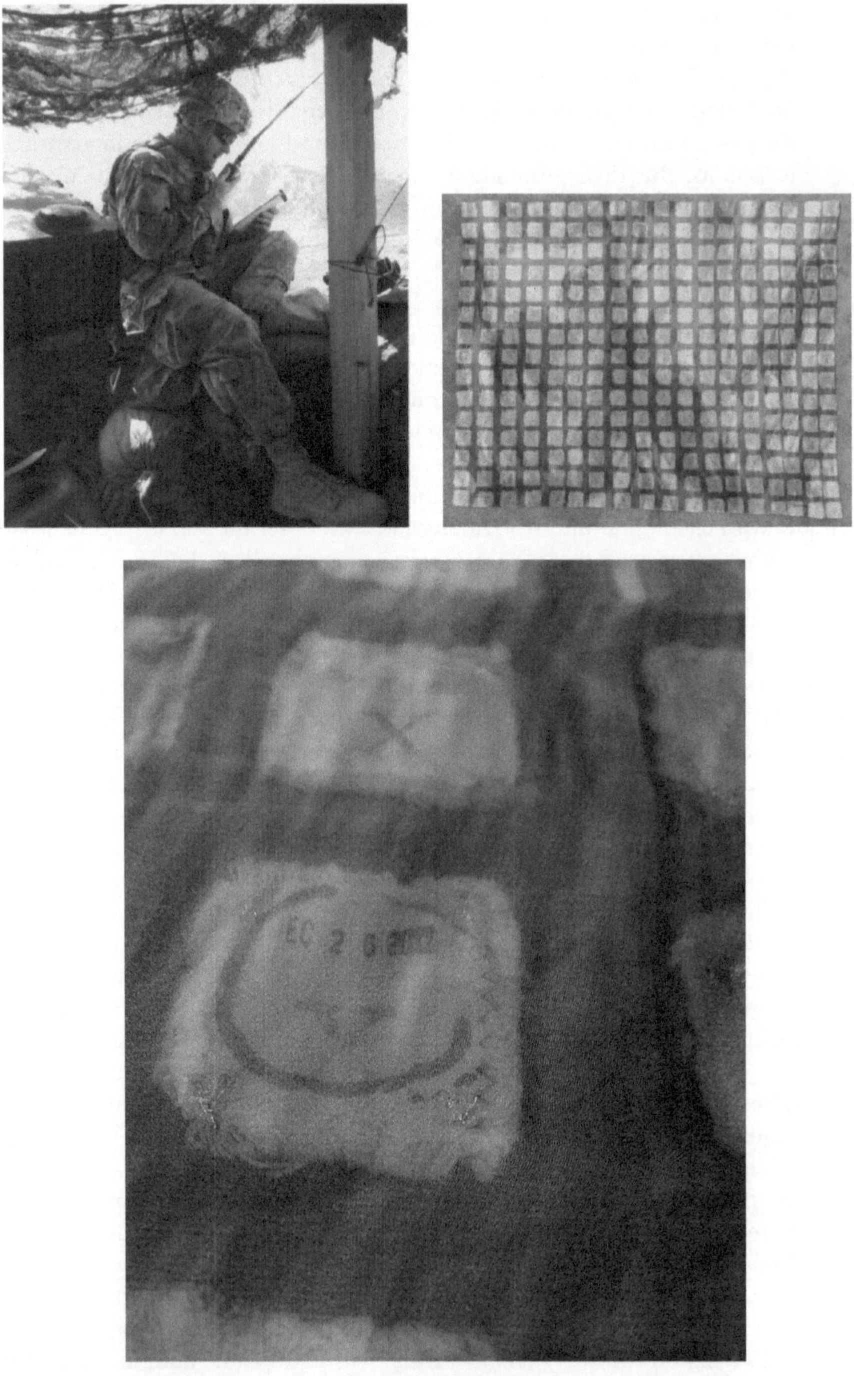

Figure 4.45 Kathi's deployment quilt. Top left: Kathi's son. Top right: The entire quilt, measuring 46″ × 39″. Bottom: A close-up of an X. (Printed with permission.)

Pébéo Paints: Cotton and Silk

Admittedly, I love all of the Pébéo products that I have tried. As can be seen in Figure 4.38, I have incorporated the paints on cotton and muslin to create my own creatures whether they are added to quilts, pillows, or clothing. There is also a Pébéo line for silk paints, which I will cover shortly. The top-left image of Figure 4.46 illustrates Pébéo being painted on muslin; the top-right image shows a finished pillow created with Pébéo paints and quilted; the bottom images illustrate Pébéo painted on yoga pants for one of my closest friends (so she can wear her dog to yoga).

Working with silk and Pébéo or Jacquard Silk paints is a wonderful medium to use with patients. Like the Pébéo Vitrea and Porcelaine tubes (Figure 4.39), Pébéo also makes similar tubes for working on clothing. They come in a variety of formats, from their traditional Pébéo gutta resist tubes to their Setacolor 3D

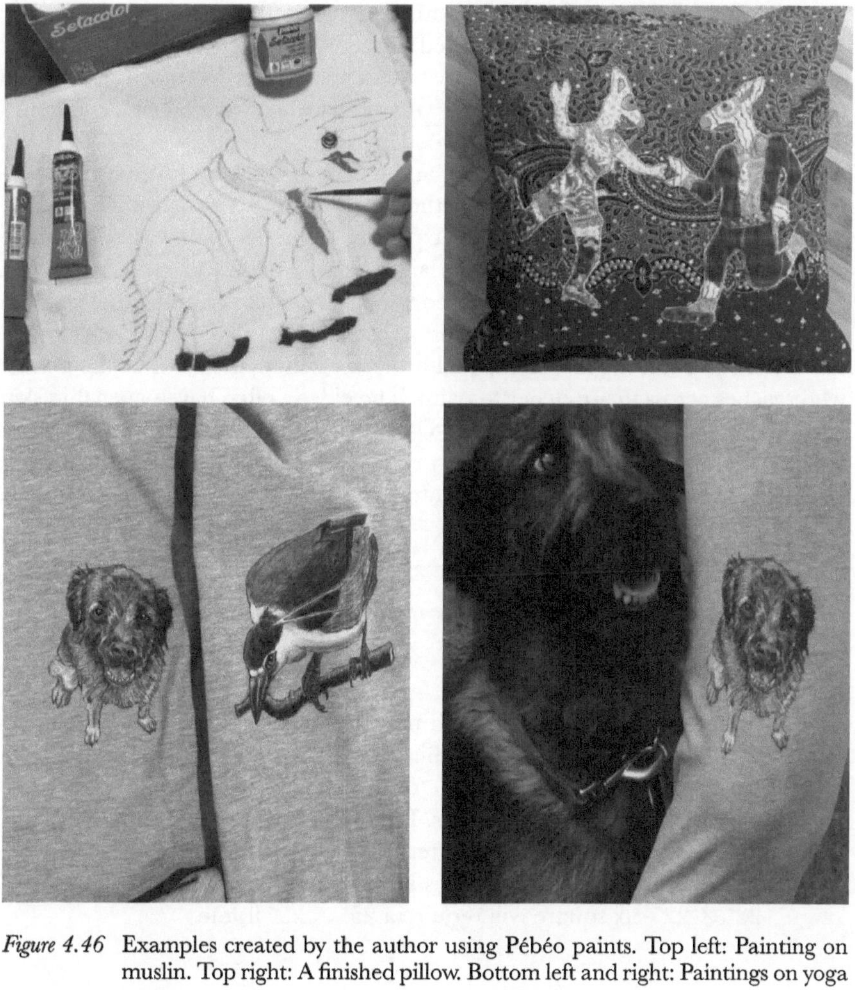

Figure 4.46 Examples created by the author using Pébéo paints. Top left: Painting on muslin. Top right: A finished pillow. Bottom left and right: Paintings on yoga pants.

resist tubes. These tubes range in colors from their Brod'Line Effect, to Gloss, Metal, Glitter, and Phosphorescent. These resists can create very interesting effects on any kind of fabric, including silk. Dharma Trading Co. sells a wealth of materials, from cotton to silk clothing, that can be dyed and hand painted with Pébéo resists. I have found using silk paints to be very successful when working with all kinds of populations. For the elderly, the artistic process provides creative pleasure and social connectedness and reaffirms capabilities. For children, it allows for spontaneous freedom and wearable items. The versatility of the medium allows for use with many populations. One of my former students, Maureen Stathis, a brilliant artist and art therapist, first introduced me to silk as part of a class presentation. (And I have been hooked on it ever since!) She aptly wrote, "Silk painting is a metaphor for life, as you have little control over the fluidity of the medium. The resist represents barriers and obstacles faced in everyday life" (Stathis, 2013). Truer than true.

The mechanics involved in painting a silk scarf can be as simple as ironing the silk onto freezer paper (and, should you wish, using the tubes for resist) before applying the silk paints or as complicated as making a stretcher out of wood and/or PVC tubing. The first method is great to use for groups if you do not have the money or time to make a stretcher and works great when working with children. I opt to use PVC tubing (as opposed to wooden frames) since it is portable (the PVC can be taken apart at the PVC elbows) and is easy to reach over if you are working in a group. The old-fashioned method of creating a wooden frame at least 3″ larger than the size of your silk piece has two inherent problems: (1) storage (especially if the size of the silk is very large); and (2) the use of nails. When you create a stretcher out of wood, you need to place nails all around so that you can suspend elastic bands on the nail heads and stretch the silk. When working with the elderly, you run the risk of the nail heads scratching the arms of the person who reaches across the stretcher to paint. The elderly often have paper-thin skin and this is a risk that I prefer to avoid. Using PVC is much kinder and while initially it may be more expensive, it is worth the extra cost. Below are instructions on how to create a stretcher whether you are using a wooden frame or PVC tubing.

Painting Silk Scarves and Banners

Making a Stretcher

- A frame is required to stretch the silk. The silk must be stretched tightly and suspended above the work surface for finishing.
- For stretching, create a custom frame with 1″ × 2″ wooden pieces or use artist canvas stretcher bars. Preferably, PVC tubing can be used as a safe and more portable alternative.
- Frames should be a few inches larger than the silk. For example, a 22″ × 22″ silk square will require a 25″ × 25″ frame.

- Around the entire frame, if using wood, hammer in small nails approximately 3″ to 4″ apart, leaving ¼″ of the nail head exposed.
- If you are using PVC, simply stretch an elastic band around the PVC tubing, and attach one end of a safety pin to the elastic band and the other to the silk.

Supplies Needed

- Frame, safety pins, rubber bands, foam or paint brushes, iron, Washable Wonder marker
- Fabric: 8mm Habotai silk
- Resist: Pébéo gutta resist tubes or Pébéo Setacolor 3D resist tubes
- Paints: Jacquard Dye-Na-Flow silk paint or Pébéo silk paint.

Stretching Silk on a Frame

1 Using safety pins and rubber bands, stretch the silk onto the frame.
2 Pin the safety pins evenly around the perimeter of the scarf approximately 2″ to 3″ apart.
3 Thread a rubber band through each safety pin, placing the end loops of the rubber band over the nail heads in the frame or around the PVC tubing if you are using that stretcher method. Check that the suspended silk is taut.

Serti Technique

1 Using a Washable Wonder fabric marker, draw your design onto the silk.
2 Apply resist to the design and let it dry. (Resist can be applied with a rubber stamp, bottle tip, brush, etc.) Use Pébéo gutta resist markers (to create a barrier for the silk paint when it flows) or Pébéo Setacolor 3D tubes.
3 Dip your brush into each color sparingly and apply, moving from lighter colors to darker. Let the colors blend.
4 Coarse salt and drops of rubbing alcohol may be applied to the wet dye to add texture.
5 Allow to dry for 24 hours.
6 Remove the silk from the frame and iron for five minutes (on silk setting) per section. Use the hottest setting allowed that does not result in burning the silk. The silk usually will not burn at the highest setting unless the iron remains stationary. The hotter the iron, the more the silk fibers mesh with the dyes and retain color intensity.
7 Wash the silk to remove sediment and clear water-based resist, and re-iron.

(N.B.: Make sure to suggest that patients dress appropriately for the art studio. These dyes are permanent and can damage clothing.)

The top-left image in Figure 4.47 illustrates a group of adults creating a banner using a wooden frame with elastic bands stretched over the nail heads. The image on the middle left shows a silk handkerchief created by the author being stretched over a PVC frame, with the finished product shown in the bottom-left

Figure 4.47 Top left: Using a wooden-framed stretcher for silk painting. Middle left: Using a PVC-framed stretcher for silk painting. Bottom left: The finished silk handkerchief on the PVC-framed stretcher. Top right and bottom right: Examples of completed silk scarves created by the author.

image. Note that this example also involved a Citra Solv photo transfer onto the silk prior to painting using the Serti silk-painting technique (using resists to stop the flow of silk paint). The top-right image illustrates a completed scarf created by the author again using a Citra Solv photo transfer onto the silk piece. In the bottom-right image is an example of another silk scarf created by the author, using only the Serti method.

The Case of T

Every once in a while, a case comes along where you get to work with someone particularly gifted. I briefly treated this talented 24-year-old woman and part of this case was presented at the 47th annual American Art Therapy Association Conference (Horovitz, 2016a). This case will be covered in depth in the next section on digital applications since the patient was seen both online (via my Breakthrough online site, http://drellenghorovitz.breakthrough.com) and in person in my private practice.

T was exceptionally talented, sketched between sessions, and openly shared her journal entries with me. When she entered treatment, she was openly weepy, dealing with mourning and loss issues, and depressed. Because she was open to working with a variety of materials, after having to put her pet dog to sleep during our treatment, I thought that it might help her in the grieving process if she created a silk handkerchief with an image of "Butch" (pseudonym) on it. So she sent a few digital files to me while we were in session and then after printing them out, she decided to use the image on the left of Figure 4.48. The image on the right shows how Butch is embedded on the finished handkerchief as well as on the background of her backyard where he is buried. Having this permanent image of Butch imprinted on her beautiful silk handkerchief served both as a comfort to T and as a transitional object for her to carry around during the mourning process (Winnicott, 1953). (For clarification for the reader, the image

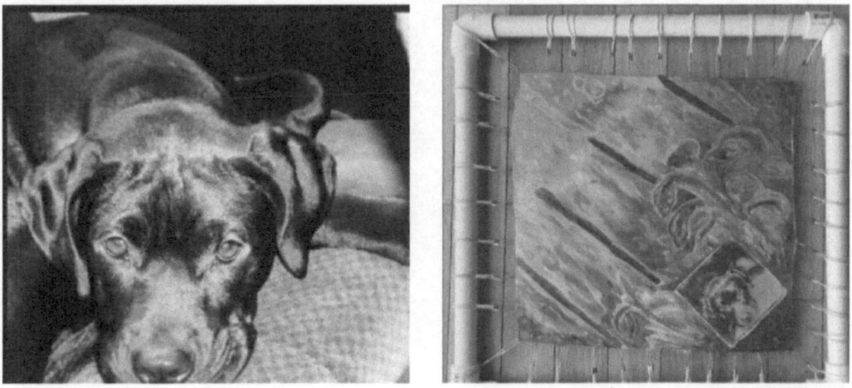

Figure 4.48 Butch on a silk handkerchief created by T, a 24-year-old patient struggling with mourning and loss issues as well as depression. (Printed with permission.)

of Butch was transferred onto the silk using the Citra Solv transfer method, then outlined with Pébéo transparent gutta paint (to create a resist and barrier), and finally painted with Pébéo silk paints before ironing.)

Felting

In addition to painting on silk, quilting, and sewing, felting and knitting deserve particular mention. I first learned about stress balls made from felting from one of my German exchange students, Martina Reiss. She arrived from Germany and gave me a stress ball, which I placed in the pocket of my art smock, where it lived for years. Every time I squeezed it, it reminded me of Martina and the memories that I had of her as a student. Fortunately, we are still in touch, as she is a colleague; we exchange cards and gifts on a regular basis and message each other through Facebook.

While I didn't think much about felting as an application, it came up again in 2012, when my students, (now colleagues) Alicia Morley, Eleanor Poore, Michele Price, and Kelsey Wall presented on felting during one of the classes that I taught. While this is an artform in and of itself, I will only skim the possibilities of this amazing medium and highlight the possibilities of painting with felted wool featuring the artwork of Demaris Verzulli. Her felted silk scarf (featured in Figure 4.49) is *nuno*, which means "fabric" in Japanese. It is created using silk and wool together to make a fabric. In the case of this scarf, it is a layer of fine merino wool sandwiched between two layers of silk. But *nuno* can be thick and solid too, such as for a bag, a purse, or clothing. The wool shrinks but the silk doesn't, and the difference results in a crinkly silk surface. It is extremely time intensive to create such scarves by marrying the two fabrics (silk and merino wool) into one.

Figure 4.49 Felt artwork courtesy of professional artist Demaris Verzulli. Left: An image of a fox created using felt. Right: A *nuno* felt scarf. (Printed with permission.)

Below, I will briefly outline the art of making stress balls (a much quicker process) as presented to me by art therapists Morley, Poore, Price, and Wall.

Making Felt Stress Balls

Supplies Needed

- Merino wool
- Liquid dishwashing soap
- Hot water
- Towels
- Bowl/tray.

Method

1. Prepare hot and soapy water in the bowl/tray.
2. Gently pull off wool from the strand. Set your hands wide apart while holding strand; fibers will easily separate this way.
3. Pull apart small pieces.
4. Form the wool into a ball.
5. Dip the ball into hot and soapy water.
6. Roll the ball gently in the palm of your hands; repeat until the ball feels more dense. If in doubt, do it more. You want a solid core. (It may take as long as ten minutes of rolling before your ball starts to feel dense.)
7. Continue to add small pieces of wool to make the ball larger. Always dip it in hot and soapy water! Replace the water if necessary. Hot and soapy water is the key to getting the fibers to lock together. When your ball is dense and the size you wish, you can add decorative strands.
8. Gently rub the strips of wool into your ball.
9. Run the ball under cold water and squeeze to remove excess soap; the ball may shrink a little.
10. Let it sit to dry (for at least 24 hours). Decorate with ribbon/beads or the like when ready!

For more ideas, I suggest that the reader go to Pinterest and check out the Needle and Wet Felting pages for inspiration (https://www.pinterest.com/simocallioni/needle-and-wet-felting). *(Warning: Pinterest can be highly addictive. But you can be inspired and learn a ton from other artists and people "pinning" their favorite ideas and sites.)*

Felt fabric can also be used in its more traditional fashion and purchased from a store to create puppets, masks – well, pretty much anything you can think of. The same patient who painted the glass products illustrated in Figure 4.40 also

Figure 4.50 Left: Felt balls and photo by art therapist Martina Reiss. Right: Embellished felt balls from http://fabicontusmanos.blogspot.co.uk/2009/09. (Printed with permission.)

Figure 4.51 Top left: A sample felt toy created by the author. Top right and bottom: Felt toys created by a 35-year-old woman with post-partum depression, anxiety, physical issues, and PTSD. (Printed with permission.)

Table 4.2 Pre- and post-test DASS-21 results for the 35-year-old woman.

PRE-TEST

DASS-21	*Score*	*Normal*	*Mild*	*Moderate*	*Severe*	*Extremely Severe*
Depression	24				Severe	
Anxiety	24					Extremely Severe
Stress	28				Severe	

POST-TEST

DASS-21	*Score*	*Normal*	*Mild*	*Moderate*	*Severe*	*Extremely Severe*
Depression	22				Severe	
Anxiety	20					Extremely Severe
Stress	20			Moderate		

created the toys shown in the top-right and bottom images of Figure 4.51. This woman, who struggled with post-partum depression, anxiety, physical issues, and PTSD, created these adorable felt toys for her two toddlers. Several weeks passed as she created the toys. Most of the work was completed with a sewing machine. Some of the work was finished by hand. Considering that this patient had never used a sewing machine before, she caught on very quickly. I created the felt toy in the top-left image as an example. The two felt toys (top-right image) were for her two boys, as were the simple felted sock puppets (bottom images). Soon after, we talked about making curtains for her boys' rooms. While she never completed that project, a spark was ignited. While this woman still struggles with post-partum depression, anxiety, physical issues, and PTSD, one can see from her pre-test/post-test scores on the DASS-21 (Depression Anxiety Stress Scale) that doing these simple handicrafts lowered her anxiety, stress, and depression (Table 4.2). While often I incorporate yoga therapy in our sessions, these scores only reflect work in art therapy and psychotherapy for that session when the puppets were completed. More about the DASS-21 will be covered in the next section on digital applications (Horovitz, 2014a, 2016a, forthcoming).

Knitting

Beyond the writings of Collier (2011a), Reynolds (1999, 2000, 2002) and Duffy (2007) specifically talked about a therapeutic technique that incorporated a knitting program in order to successfully facilitate discussions, improve the milieu, and moderate stress and emotions, both for inpatient and outpatient clients.

Corkhill et al. (2014) explored how knitting contributed to well-being at the 2012 conference "In the Loop 3: The Voices of Knitting." The outcome was their paper "Knitting and Well-being" (2014): while the voices are diverse, so too are the many ways in which knitting can contribute to our well-being today.

Again, I used knitting with the same woman whose artwork is shown in Figures 4.40 and 4.51. While she found this learning curve to be difficult at best, I offered it to her to reduce her anxiety since there had been numerous sources in the literature that contributed to this idea. Because she also struggled with eating disorders, I decided to employ this medium based on the work of Clave-Brule et al. (2009). Their research suggested that performing a visuospatial task reduces the perceived intensity of self-image. Subjects were asked to report the qualitative effects of knitting on their psychological state using a self-report questionnaire. Results indicated a subjective reduction in anxious preoccupation when knitting. In particular, 28 of 38 (women) (74%) reported decreased intensity of fears and thoughts and preoccupations with eating, 28 of 38 (74%) reported a calming and therapeutic effect, and 20 of 38 (53%) reported satisfaction, pride, and a sense of accomplishment in the resulting work.

The Case of H

H was a patient who suffered from trichotillomania. According to the OCD Center of Los Angeles:

> The defining characteristic of Trichotillomania is the recurrent, compulsive pulling out of one's own hair, resulting in observable hair loss. Usually, but not always, the scalp and/or face are the primary locations for hair pulling. While the most common hair pulling sites are the scalp, eyebrows, and eyelashes, Trichotillomania may involve any part of the body with hair. Less common locations for hair pulling include the pubic area, perirectal region, arms, chest, and legs. An individual with Trichotillomania may use his or her fingernails, as well as tweezers, pins, or other mechanical devices. In severe cases, Trichotillomania can result in permanent hair loss or skin damage.
>
> Often, but not always, Trichotillomania episodes are preceded by a high level of tension and a strong "urge." Likewise, hair pulling is usually, but not always, followed by a sensation of relief or pleasure. Hair pulling is usually done alone, often while watching TV, reading, talking on the phone, driving, or while grooming in the bathroom. A Trichotillomania episode may be triggered by a negative mood state or occur in response to stress, but may also occur while an individual is calm and relaxed. Sometimes hair pulling is done as a conscious behavior, but it is frequently done as an unconscious habit.
>
> (www.ocdla.com/trichotillomania.html)

Because this case was complicated by the fact that H was adopted from Vietnam, it is also important to understand the culture of the Vietnamese population. According to Cerquone (1986) and Yarborough (2005), the Vietnamese value Vietnamese fathers as socially pure, whereas American fathers are not valued in the same way; as a consequence, Amerasian children are not valued in the same manner as Vietnamese children. Post-Vietnam, most Amerasians arrived in the US as unaccompanied minors. These children struggled with issues of abandonment, loss, coping with a different language and culture, and pervasive racial discrimination.

A look at H's genogram clearly explains her background and presenting symptoms.

The first few months of therapy, I just sat with H and sipped tea until a therapeutic alliance was established. After the initial adjustment, all art therapy tests indicated that H suffered from depression and lack of nurturance. Overall, her developmental age placed the 11-year-old H at the lower end of the gang age, 9 years old according to Lowenfeld and Brittain (1975) and as indicated in her KFD (Kinetic Family Drawing). Figure 4.53 shows H's KFD titled "waiting for my foster family to come and get me." H is alone in the bottom left, suggesting separation and abandonment issues.

One day, H wandered over toward my desk and took an interest in knitting. As a result, knitting lessons began, and H's trichotillomania disappeared when she engaged in knitting. As a result, she was allowed to take the needles and her work back to her residential cottage. Soon, H was open to drawing and other art materials. However, H continued to struggle with her familial issues and became more withdrawn when visiting her foster family. One day, H received a long-awaited reply letter from her foster grandmother in Vietnam. She arrived to art therapy with her half-knitted sweater, placed it on the table, and stated,

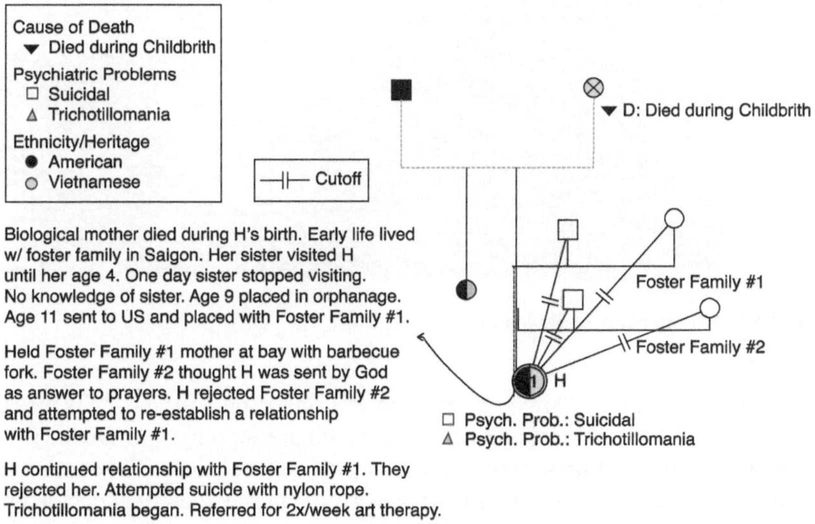

Figure 4.52 H's genogram and background. (Printed with permission.)

Figure 4.53 H's KFD. (Printed with permission.)

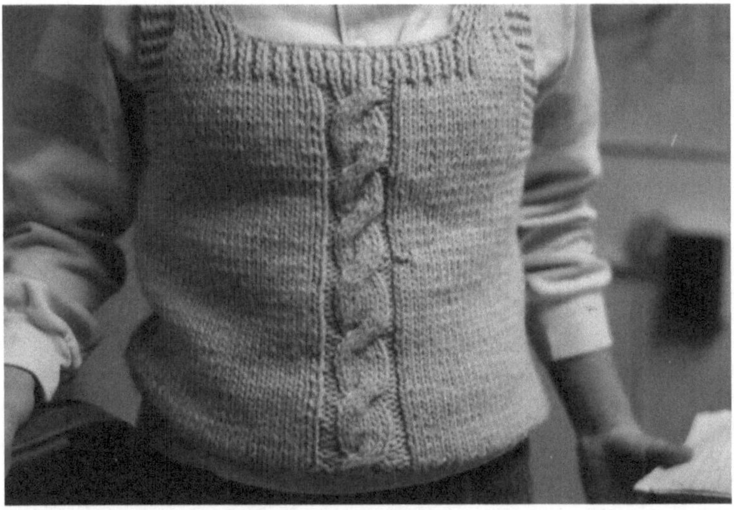

Figure 4.54 H in her finished sweater.

"I no come to art therapy anymore, give my knitting to another girl." Six weeks elapsed with no artwork and again H sat in silence sipping tea. During the seventh month of treatment, family art therapy finally began, and H continued knitting her sweater. For an art therapy project, the family members decided to make a hooked rug together. During that family art therapy session, the family members were also instructed to hug daily. Communication barriers finally broke down and bonding with the foster family renewed. Soon, H was well enough to be discharged to the foster family.

At termination, H began to crochet a blanket for herself. As she left, loaded down with art supplies, her portfolio, and knitting materials, she once again appeared to be an unaccompanied refugee minor; yet the trichotillomania had stopped and there was hope as she started her life with her new family that perhaps now she would be equipped to weave a new chapter in her life.

Population Benefits and Contraindications

As can be seen throughout this section on threaded applications and healing, hand-worked needle crafting – be it painting on fabric, sewing, quilting, felting, knitting, or using like materials – has wide applications with a variety of populations. This section discussed the use of these media by patients ranging from school-aged children to adults, with a variety of etiologies: trichotillomania, anxiety, depression, stress, and even blindness. While working with some media (such as knitting) can cause frustration (a cautionary note since this may be contraindicated for those with OCD – obsessive compulsive disorder with traits of perfectionism), for the most part, these media have wide applications for healing and, in some instances (such as the case of H), can be truly life-saving.

Digital Applications for a Twenty-First-Century Palette

Telehealth Applications and Research

Before we look at the digital applications available, first we need to discuss the ethics of such topics as telehealth. I have discussed this at great length (Horovitz, 2016a, forthcoming) and I urge the reader to read the referenced material as well as the work of Garner (2016). But I will summarize: as practitioners, it has often been suggested that we follow certain guidelines when working with patients concerning the assessments that we use. With the advent of the digital age, apps are being used by hospitals for intakes (prior to examination). Similarly, art therapy practitioners are ascertaining mood and creative information via such apps as the DASS-21 (Depression Anxiety Stress Scale) and Paper 53 (Horovitz, 2014a, 2014b, 2015a, 2015b, 2015c, 2016a). Apps such as the DASS-21 are being employed by a variety of telehealth companies such as HealthLinkNow, Breakthrough, and EverBliss, just to name a few (Stross, 2011). Although the term "telehealth" more broadly can encompass a variety of communication techniques including telephone, email, text, and remote monitoring, telemedicine can include the provision of mental health diagnostic, therapeutic, or management services via real-time, interactive video conferencing and/or using apps such as Paper 53 and the DASS-21 prior to and between sessions to measure change over time and the efficacy of any kind of therapeutic treatment. I use both of these apps in my video telehealth practice through Breakthrough. While there are other companies out there (EverBliss, etc.), Breakthrough uses several items that make it the standout for telemedicine care and is HIPAA compliant. The regulations and laws to establish the ground rules for telepsychiatry/clinical practice are the same standards of care existing for face-to-face (F2F) patient care (Grady et al., 2009).

Briefly, research on telemedicine suggests that: (1) telemedicine has more than 50 years of history of providing medical care to patients via technology in distant and remote locations; (2) the provision of behavioral health care is one of the earliest and most common healthcare specialties offered via telemedicine; (3) psychiatry and other behavioral health services are the most frequent type of telemedicine after radiology; (4) recent improvements in technology cost and quality have made deployment possible for the routine practice of medicine; and (5) the empirical base of telehealth mental health consistently shows that diagnostic accuracy and treatment efficacy is equivalent to F2F for most populations and settings (Fishkind & Cuyler, 2013; Grady et al., 2009; Yellowlees et al., 2010). Given the increasing use of the internet, telehealth has extraordinary possibilities and including creative art therapists in this arena is both timely and necessary to offer avenues that go beyond verbal psychotherapy (Garner, 2016; Horovitz, 2014a, 2014b, 2015a, 2015b, 2015c, 2016a, forthcoming).

While telehealth might not yet be a part of your therapist toolbox, it is clearly part of the digital future. Although research indicates that there have been no known cases where telemedicine guidelines have been incorporated into a legal case, one certainly will arise – hopefully to provide evidence regarding the safety and efficacy of telemedicine rather than the opposite.

Practice guidelines for telemedicine are important and valuable for helping insure effective and safe delivery of quality healthcare. Existing practice guidelines have been well received by the telemedicine community and are being adopted in numerous practices. Some state medical boards have specifically incorporated American Telehealth Association (ATA) practice guidelines into their rules or proposed rules (e.g., New York, North Carolina, Oklahoma, and Pennsylvania). Basically, they state that physicians must practice telemedicine in compliance with standards endorsed by the ATA (Krupinski et al., 2010; Krupinski & Bernard, 2014). For the near future, we will continue to need guidelines developed for individual sub-specialties such as art therapy. To some extent, this is needed to help convince funders and legislators that telemedicine is just another way to provide patient care and thus should be reimbursed just like any other medical encounter without excessive regulations. And in fact, as the world becomes increasingly digital, we need to view telemedicine as yet another platform (and palette) for operating towards a wellness construct.

Paper 53

In one of my recent books (Horovitz, 2014a), I wrote about Paper 53 since I had been presenting on its use for a few years (Horovitz, 2014b, 2015a, 2015b, 2015c, 2016a). With current technological advancements and ease of access to graphics and photography programs, any individual with a smartphone, tablet, or laptop can now create remarkable artwork with the touch of a button. You can take an image created on a tablet (iPad), using the Paper 53 app, and then send it to a smartphone (iPhone) or computer for further manipulation using PS Express, a smartphone app, Photoshop, or a number of other tools available. The final image can be shared and posted to millions of users who can create yet another version of this original sketch. (The same thing can be done with any digital image.) And if you want to take that same image into software programs as I have done (Horovitz, 2011), the possibilities are endless. But to what end?

While these programs might be appealing for a variety of reasons, such as using them in restrictive medical environments when conducting medical art therapy, the fine and gross motor skills required when working with materials such as real pencils, paint, cameras, and indeed three-dimensional materials are not developed or even lost in this capacity. (For example, some children and others have lost their ability to write since in many educational systems in the US cursive is no longer taught!) Still, one *needs* to add this to the arsenal that is out there. I have been using the Paper 53 app along with a stylus and my iPad (the app is soon to be available on other platforms) in order to navigate medical situations that restrict the use of such media. Examples of where this technological tool could be employed are chemotherapy units, dialysis units, and post-operative units (such as an ICU). In fact, the artwork distilled from such sessions can be output into a Moleskine journal. Another less expensive option would be to create a screenshot from the image (which yields about 1 megabyte of information) and print the result onto two- and three-dimensional surfaces.

According to Malchiodi (2012a), there is even a specific art therapy app, which the art therapy assessment Facebook community is pooh-poohing. To read more about the app, I would refer the reader to Malchiodi's blog in *Psychology Today* (www.psychologytoday.com/blog/arts-and-health/201202/art-therapy-there-s-app).

Ultimately, such choices lie with the art therapist and I presented on this at the most recent American Art Therapy Association Conference (Horovitz, 2016a). There are good reasons for embracing both old and new technologies. But I urge the reader to be mindful of the reason that art therapy emerged in the first place. One can only imagine how my mentor, the great Edith Kramer, would frown upon such electronic outlets. Technology both advances and distances us from our roots. And therein lies the rub.

Case Study Using the DASS-21 and Paper 53

I worked for 16 sessions with an extremely complicated case, that of T. While occasionally I saw one or two siblings (after intake with Mom R), Momma B was uninvolved in any of the sessions and T's mother, Mom R, was involved in all sessions, be they yoga therapy, art therapy, or a combination of the two. The genogram shown in Figure 4.55 clearly sums up the presenting symptoms of this very convoluted case.

Beyond the obvious history of this child and the problems with which he struggled, T was extremely aggressive towards all of the members of his household and was exceptionally self-injurious (for example, biting his fingers and toes until they bled). Indeed, I communicated with his psychiatrist when his self-injurious behavior turned to suicidal ideation during one of our sessions (T threatened to cut off his penis so he wouldn't grow up).

Because T had bombed out of so many therapists' offices, I agreed to treat this family as long as I could have continual contact with his psychiatrist (who was very grateful that I agreed to work with this child). My methodology combined yoga therapy and art therapy with the mother/child dyad. I also conducted the DASS-21 before and after each session to monitor the efficacy of our work. I shared the results with T and his mother every session. Because T had terrible hygiene and often came to the session dirty, I decided to invoke the *yamas* and *niyamas* (the do's and the don'ts) of yoga principles. One of those doctrines is *saucha*, which refers to purity of mind, body, and speech. Because the family was highly religious, I also tied the concept of *saucha* to Jesus and the washing of his feet, thus tying into their cultural belief systems. I purchased some basins at a local dollar store; at the outset of each session, I had T and his mother wash each other's feet. It became a lovely ritual and allowed for casual banter and catch-up from the previous session. It also allowed me to conduct the DASS-21 (pre-session) and tie this into T's need to improve his hygiene and take a shower more than once a month. I also gave T and his mother homework to do between our sessions. For example, after Session 2, their homework was as follows.

Intention

1. Mom R: To have a calm week.
2. T: To love my mother better and not treat her so harshly.

(My intention was that T would learn to also love himself more.)

Take Home Practice

1. T should substitute a pen at school and a binky at home instead of chewing hands and toes.
2. T should use the hula-hoop (which we had made during Session 2) and practice *dhi rhi ha*, a yoga posture that releases energy in an appropriate manner.

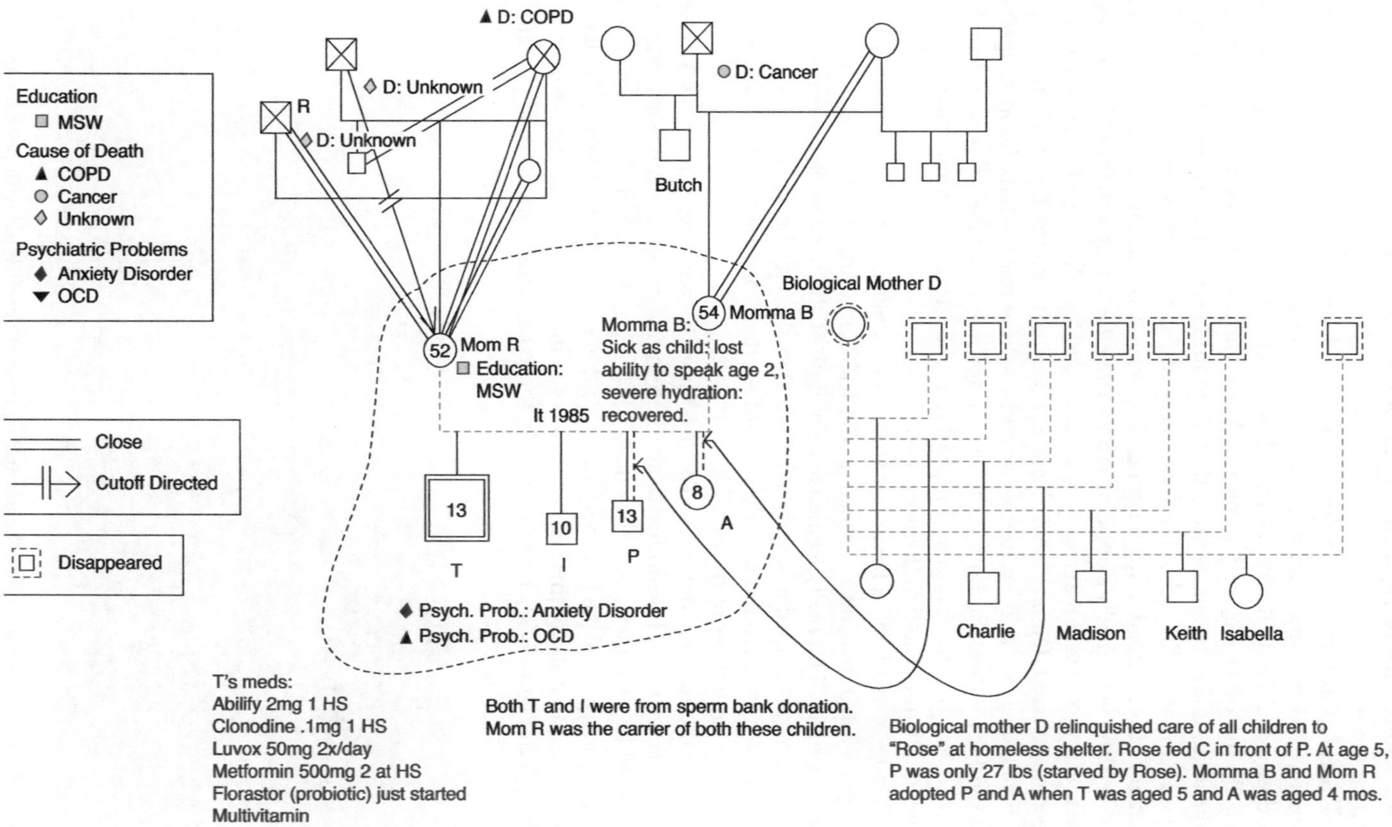

Figure 4.55 T's genogram. (Printed with permission.)

So let's speed ahead to Session 12, where I employed the DASS-21 (pre- and post-session), yoga therapy, and art therapy in the form of using the Paper 53 app on the iPad.

T arrived in tears, screaming at the top of his lungs that he just wanted someone to "give [him] a break." I had him come into the therapy room and sit down, and handed him tissues. Mom R was attending to a cell phone call outside the office before joining us. Apparently, the Committee on Special Education (CSE) recommended that T go into residential treatment because he was not attending school at least every other day and/or working towards that goal. As I helped T regain control by way of breathing exercises, Mom R entered and was equally exasperated regarding the fallout with the CSE. During the meeting, she said that she stepped back and let others talk for her when she became agitated. Despite all of this, we proceeded with the DASS-21 (pre-test). T switched gears and excitedly wanted to show me his hula-hoop progress (as did his mother). So both hula-hooped for a few minutes. T was extremely excited so I met his mood and helped him get into a headstand since he was having difficulty calming (Figure 4.56).

Post-headstand and a few other yoga poses, I placed both T and his mother in *vipariti karini* (placing their legs up the wall and using the yoga belts to hold them upright). This really seemed to calm both of them down. Because the hour was waning, I decided to use the iPad(s) for art therapy. I gave them a directive to create artwork around how they would see themselves in the upcoming week given the latest news from the CSE.

Using the marker tool in the Paper 53 app, T made everything black, save a small corner that his mother talked him into leaving open since she wished he could be "happier" and "less dark." However, T made it clear that he felt pretty grim most of the time despite his mother's desire for him to be otherwise. (She stated that she wished his artwork could be "all light with just a corner of black.") In Figure 4.57, T's artwork is on the left and his mother's is on the right.

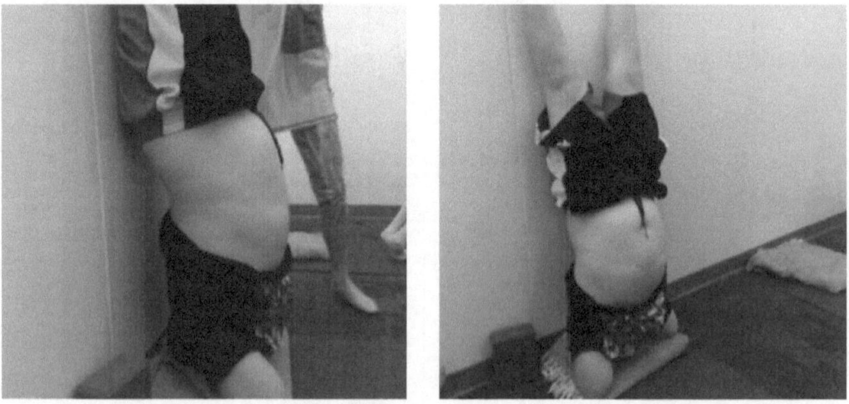

Figure 4.56 T is assisted into a headstand by the author. (Printed with permission.)

Figure 4.57 Artwork created by T and his mother using the Paper 53 app on the iPad(s).

Meanwhile, Mom R described her artwork in the following manner: "The red lines shooting out from the center are the surprises that occur and are unexpected; the black snake-like image in the center represents the meanderings of what I have to deal with."

During the session, T proudly shared that he had showered that day, but several times during the session, his mother had to tell him that he was "invading" her personal space. She also called him out on his inappropriate blurting out of information (thinking and then talking as if his mother knew what he was thinking about – Mom R and T called this "T speak"). We talked about ways in which T could be more mindful and communicative as well as less interruptive. They both left in much better shape than when they arrived. The DASS-21 results post-session (Table 4.3) clearly demonstrated the improvement in that session and how much T had calmed down from the beginning of the session (when he arrived screaming and in tears).

Sharing the DASS-21 results with T and his mother was useful in that they could actually see their own improvement within sessions and if scores elevated (unlike in this session), we were also able to talk about what was causing increases in depression, stress, and/or anxiety. Furthermore, I charted their results, and in Table 4.4 one can see pre- and post-tests on the DASS-21 for two sessions: February 5, 2015, and near our termination session, April 2, 2015. What was extraordinary was how much T's results had changed over just a few months.

Table 4.3 Pre- and post-test DASS-21 results for T and Mom R.

PRE-TEST on February 12, 2015
T's Results

DASS-21	*Score*	*Normal*	*Mild*	*Moderate*	*Severe*	*Extremely Severe*
Depression	42					Extremely Severe
Anxiety	24					Extremely Severe
Stress	42					Extremely Severe

POST-TEST on February 12, 2015
T's Results

DASS-21	*Score*	*Normal*	*Mild*	*Moderate*	*Severe*	*Extremely Severe*
Depression	14			Moderate		
Anxiety	14			Moderate		
Stress	26				Severe	

PRE-TEST on February 12, 2015
Mom R's Results

DASS-21	*Score*	*Normal*	*Mild*	*Moderate*	*Severe*	*Extremely Severe*
Depression	4	Normal				
Anxiety	14			Moderate		
Stress	26				Severe	

POST-TEST on February 12, 2015
Mom R's Results

DASS-21	*Score*	*Normal*	*Mild*	*Moderate*	*Severe*	*Extremely Severe*
Depression	2	Normal				
Anxiety	2	Normal				
Stress	4	Normal				

Table 4.4 Comparative table of pre- and post-test DASS-21 results for T and Mom R.

Date	*Age*	*Sex*	*Dx*	*Pre-test*	*Pre-test*	*Pre-test*	*Post-test*	*Post-test*	*Post-test*
				Depression	*Anxiety*	*Stress*	*Depression*	*Anxiety*	*Stress*
2/5/15	11	M	Bipolar PTSD	30 Extremely Severe	18 Severe	42 Extremely Severe	42 Extremely Severe	24 Extremely Severe	40 Extremely Severe
2/5/15	52	F	N/A	2 Normal	2 Normal	16 Mild	0 Normal	0 Normal	2 Normal
4/2/15	11	M	Bipolar PTSD	0 Normal	0 Normal	6 Normal	0 Normal	0 Normal	0 Normal
4/2/15	52	F	N/A	8 Normal	6 Normal	12 Normal	0 Normal	0 Normal	4 Normal

Prior to termination in an email to me dated April 9, 2015, Mom R wrote:

> Out of the blue "T" had this to say:
>
> > *"Mommy I'm getting better. I've been working harder than I ever have. I feel like a normal, happy child. Wow – all the things I've been missing out on. Having fun, enjoying my life. I'm doing things I've always wanted. I'm going out. I am happy. I don't feel the pressure to do bad things. I don't have the thoughts pressuring me to do bad things."*
>
> Wow. This really warmed me to the core. Something is going right.

It warmed me to the core, too.

BetterMind BetterWorld Healthcare App

Recently, while searching for new applications, I discovered the motherlode of all applications: the BetterMind BetterWorld Healthcare app. You can learn more about it at: www.betterworldhealthcare.com.

Brendan O'Shea, the founder and president of the company, kindly allowed me to beta-test this app before its official launch. I can honestly say that it hit the jackpot. The reasons are multifold, but for starters, there are 40 psychological tests included within the application:

1. ASSQ: Autism Spectrum Screening Questionnaire
2. AUDIT: Alcohol Use Disorders Identification Test
3. CESD-R: Center for Epidemiologic Studies Depression Scale – Revised
4. ChOCI-R-P: Obsessional Compulsive Inventory – Revised
5. ChOCI-R-S: Children's Obsessional Compulsive Inventory – Revised
6. CY-BOCS: Children's Yale–Brown Obsessive Compulsive Scale
7. DASS-21: Depression Anxiety Stress Scale – Short Form
8. DASS-42: Depression Anxiety Stress Scale – Long Form
9. EAT-26: Eating Attitudes Test – 26
10. ECR-S: Experience in Close Relationship Scale
11. EPDS: Edinburgh Postnatal Depression Scale
12. FMPS: Frost Multidimensional Perfectionism Scale
13. FS: Flourishing Scale
14. GAD-7: Generalized Anxiety Disorder Scale
15. IES-R: Impact of Event Scale
16. K10: Kessler Psychological Distress Scale
17. MCQ-30: Metacognition Questionnaire – 30
18. MFQ- P: Parent Moods and Feelings Questionnaire – Parent Report
19. MFQ-S: Self Moods and Feelings Questionnaire – Self Report
20. ORT: Opioid Risk Tool
21. PCL-5: PTSD Checklist 5

22 PDSS: Panic Disorder Severity Scale
23 PHQ-9: Patient Health Questionnaire – Depression
24 PSEQ: Pain Self-Efficacy Questionnaire
25 PSWQ: Penn State Worry Questionnaire
26 RSES: Rosenberg Self-Esteem Scale
27 SADS: Social Avoidance and Distress Scale
28 SCAS-Child: Spence Children's Anxiety Scale – Child
29 SCAS-Parent: Spence Children's Anxiety Scale – Parent
30 SIAS: Social Interaction Scale
31 SPANE: Scale of Positive and Negative Experience
32 SPS: Social Phobia Scale
33 SWLS: Satisfaction with Life Scale
34 TAFS-R: Thought Action Fusion Scale – Revised
35 TSK: Tampa Scale of Kinesiophobia
36 UPPS-P: UPPS-P Impulsive Behavior Scale
37 VOCI: Vancouver Obsessional Compulsive Inventory
38 Y-BOCS: Yale–Brown Obsessive Compulsive Scale
39 Y-BOCS-SC: Y-BOCS Symptom Checklist
40 ZUNG: Self-Rating Depression Scale

The screening and assessment scales help physicians and other qualified healthcare providers to diagnose, treat, and monitor mental health illness, substance abuse, and misuse issues. Some of the mental health illnesses that the app can diagnose include depression, anxiety, psychosomatic disorders, opioid risk, alcohol dependence, bipolar disorder, perinatal depression, and ADD.

One of the best features of this app is how secure it is. Besides having a private login and password, the clinician also sets a four-digit passcode to access the application, enter information on the patient, and access patient results. With the DASS-21 app (previously mentioned), the patient can inadvertently access his/her scores/results. This is not the case with the BetterMind BetterWorld Healthcare app. Instead, it locks out the patient and the only way that information can be accessed is for the clinician to log in with his/her four-digit passcode. Besides that, the pièce de résistance is that the report is instantly generated. It can be viewed and sent to the clinician as a PDF (or a CSV file, should you care to tabulate the information for more data and research). The report can easily be converted so that the clinician can enter his/her own logo and company information in the header of the report. Indeed, documentation using the app can not only enhance patient care but also help mitigate practice risk for the clinician. To boot, it's amazingly streamlined and, in a word, brilliant.

In a recent clinical situation, it afforded me information on my patient that had not yet come up in our treatment. During our second session, I had my 23-year-old female patient take the 15-question inventory in the CESD-R (Center for Epidemiologic Studies Depression Scale – Revised). Much to my surprise, the results indicated suicidal ideation. While clearly this patient had all

Table 4.5 CESD-R sample results.

Client Information	
Client name	Case Sample 23 yo Female
Date of birth (age)	age (23)
Assessment Information	
Assessment	Center for Epidemiologic Studies Depression Scale – Revised (CESD-R)
Date administered	30 November 2016
Assessor	Dr. Ellen G. Horovitz
Time taken	1 minute 20 seconds

Results

	Raw Score	Percentile compared to adults	Percentile compared to students
Total	36	98.6	92.7

Interpretive Text

Given that this individual scored 16 or above, she is likely to be experiencing clinically significant depression. A diagnosis of Major Depressive Disorder can be made by referencing criteria set out in *DSM-5*.

This individual endorsed one or more question pertaining to suicide. It is recommended that a further risk assessment be carried out.

Compared to other symptoms of depression reported by this individual, responses indicate that she is experiencing relatively higher levels of: Guilt (Worthlessness): Questions 9, 17

Scoring and Interpretation Information

Scores are presented as total raw scores as well and two percentiles, one based on a community sample of adults and the other based on a student sample (mean age = 19.5). High scores indicate more symptoms of depression.

Further interpretation of individual responses can be done in light of the symptoms clusters of Major Depressive Disorder.

1 – Sadness (Dysphoria): Questions 2, 4, 6
2 – Loss of Interest (Anhedonia): Questions 8, 10
3 – Appetite: Questions 1, 18
4 – Sleep: Questions 5, 11, 19
5 – Thinking/Concentration: Questions 3, 20
6 – Guilt (Worthlessness): Questions 9, 17
7 – Tired (Fatigue): Questions 7, 16
8 – Movement (Agitation): Questions 12, 13
9 – Suicidal Ideation: Questions 14,15

Client Name Case Sample 23 yo Female

According to the *DSM-5* criteria, diagnosis of Major Depressive Disorder can be made if five (or more) of the above symptoms clusters are endorsed and at least one of the symptoms is either (1) depressed mood or (2) loss of interest in pleasure.

Client Responses

		Not at all / Less than 1 day	1–2 days	3–4 days	5–7 days	Nearly every day for 2 weeks
1	My appetite was poor.	**0**	**1**	**2**	**3**	**4**
2	I could not shake off the blues.	**0**	**1**	**2**	**3**	**4**
3	I had trouble keeping my mind on what I was doing.	**0**	**1**	**2**	**3**	**4**
4	I felt depressed.	**0**	**1**	**2**	**3**	**4**
5	My sleep was restless.	**0**	**1**	**2**	**3**	**4**
6	I felt sad.	**0**	**1**	**2**	**3**	**4**
7	I could not get going.	**0**	**1**	**2**	**3**	**4**
8	Nothing made me happy.	**0**	**1**	**2**	**3**	**4**
9	I felt like a bad person.	**0**	**1**	**2**	**3**	**4**
10	I lost interest in my usual activities.	**0**	**1**	**2**	**3**	**4**
11	I slept much more than usual.	**0**	**1**	**2**	**3**	**4**
12	I felt like I was moving too slowly.	**0**	**1**	**2**	**3**	**4**
13	I felt fidgety.	**0**	**1**	**2**	**3**	**4**
14	I wished I were dead.	**0**	**1**	**2**	**3**	**4**
15	I wanted to hurt myself.	**0**	**1**	**2**	**3**	**4**

of the hallmarks of clinical depression (thus the confirmation with the CESD-R), this was still an unexpected result. It allowed me to discuss my concern with the patient (in our next session) and follow up with her primary care physician (PCP) regarding my concern and the need for medication screening. Table 4.5 shows the results that were generated from this app, with identifying information of the aforementioned patient removed. In this instance, the app may have been life-saving. I was completely convinced that the app is worth its weight in gold.

At this juncture, the company has determined the price point. The final selling price has been discounted for art therapists (since I beta-tested the app) and is within reach of most clinicians. This software application is an astounding addition to track patient efficacy, outcomes, data, and research. I would highly recommend it for any clinician, whether his/her affiliation is with a hospital, school, agency, or private practice.

Population Benefits and Contraindications

As can be seen throughout this section, the advent of technology has changed the face of therapy with digital platforms such as Breakthrough and EverBliss, and apps such as Paper 53, DASS-21, and BetterMind BetterWorld Healthcare. While there are numerous digital applications available, for breadth's sake, I have focused on the ethical ramifications of communicating with patients through video applications versus F2F communications and the efficacy around both platforms. I also want to point out the importance of communicating through email and text. Communicating with patients using all of the aforementioned ways is expanding our ability to interact with them in various venues as well as outside the context of F2F or video feed (e.g., emailing and texting between sessions).

While the cases presented herein are just the tip of the iceberg in how to use digital applications, I have used digital applications since the late 1990s and presented and published my findings (Horovitz, 1999, 2011, 2014a, 2014b, 2015a, 2015b, 2015c, 2016a, forthcoming). While some populations might not be altogether comfortable using Photoshop, Paper 53, and other such programs, if the art therapist is well versed in these applications, he/she can act as a third hand and assist patients with the digital outcome. Still, there may be some patients who are steadfastly against using digital applications as a means of expression, and for those patients digital applications might be contraindicated. I have not found this to be the case and my work has encompassed the Deaf, stroke survivors, cancer survivors, emotionally disturbed children, adolescents, and adults, and then some. For medical populations, where art materials cannot be brought in (think ICU, post-operative procedures, dialysis, etc.), these applications can have enormous benefits and often can reduce stressful situations by giving patients something else to focus on besides pain and the procedure at hand. As far as the BetterMind BetterWorld Healthcare app goes, the information available to the clinician in report form is not just a time-saver but, as indicated in my case with the 23-year-old female patient, may also be a life-saver. Moreover, documentation using the app can mitigate practice risk for the practitioner. All in all, beyond its robust nature (40 diagnostic tests to date, which generate secure reports for the clinician), with the advent of electronic record keeping, this application is a must for digitally minded practitioners. *(N.B.: Practitioners need to note that the BetterMind BetterWorld Healthcare app is <u>not</u> a substitute for proper diagnosis but may indeed lead to a more informed diagnosis and better patient care.)*

References

Aristotle (2006). *On the soul.* Translated by J. A. Smith. Stilwell: Digireads.com.

Cerquone, J. (1986). Vietnam's American children. *Commonweal,* 239 (April), 45–54.

Clave-Brule, M., Mazlom, A., Park, R. J., Harbottle, E. J. C., & Birmingham, C. L. (2009). Managing anxiety disorders in eating disorders with knitting. *Eating and Weight Disorders: Studies on Anorexia, Bulimia, and Obesity, 14*(1), 1-e5.

Collier, A. F. (2011a). The well-being of women who create with textiles: Implications for art therapy. *Art Therapy: Journal of the American Art Therapy Association, 28*(3), 104–112.

Collier, A. F. (2011b). *Using textile arts and handcrafts in therapy with women: Weaving lives back together.* London: Jessica Kingsley Publishers.

Corkhill, B., Hemmings, J., Maddock, A., & Riley, J. (2014). Knitting and well-being. *Textile: Cloth and Culture, 12*(1), 34–57.

Duffy, K. (2007). Knitting as an experiential teaching method for affect management in group therapy. *Journal of Groups in Addiction Recovery, 2*(1), 67–83.

Everett, K. (2016). Personal communication, December 7, 2016.

Feen-Calligan, H., McIntyre, B., & Sands-Goldstein, M. (2009). Art therapy applications of dolls in grief recovery, identity and community service. *Art Therapy: Journal of the American Art Therapy Association, 26*(4), 167–173.

Fishkind, A., & Cuyler, R. (2013). The role of telepsychiatry. In L. S. Lun (Ed.), *Behavioral emergencies for the emergency physician* (pp. 303–307). New York, NY: Cambridge University Press.

Fryear, J. L., & Corbit, I. E. (1992). *Photo art therapy: A Jungian perspective.* Springfield, IL: Charles C. Thomas.

Garner, R. (Ed.) (2016). *Digital art therapy: Material methods and applications.* Philadelphia, PA: Jessica Kingsley Publishers.

Grady, B., Myers, K., & Nelson, E. (2009). Evidence-based practice for telemental health, American Telemedicine Association, July. Retrieved September 1, 2015 from www.americantelemed.org/docs/default-source/standards/evidence-based-practice-for-telemental-health.pdf?sfvrsn=4.

Hinz, L. (2016). Media considerations in art therapy: Directions for future research. In D. E. Gussak and M. L. Rosal (Eds.), *The Wiley handbook of art therapy* (pp. 135–145). Malden, MA: John Wiley & Sons, Ltd.

Horovitz, E. G. (1999). *A leap of faith: The call to art.* Springfield, IL: Charles C. Thomas.

Horovitz, E. G. (2005). *Art therapy as witness: A sacred guide.* Springfield, IL: Charles C. Thomas.

Horovitz, E. G. (2011). *Digital image transfer: Creating art with your photography.* New York, NY: Pixiq, Sterling Publishers.

Horovitz, E. G. (Ed.) (2014a). *The art therapists' primer: A clinical guide to writing assessments, diagnosis, and treatment* (2nd Ed). Springfield, IL: Charles C. Thomas.

Horovitz, E. G. (2014b). Family yoga therapy/art therapy with an ADD child and her family. Expressive Therapies Summit, New York, November 9, 2014.

Horovitz, E. G. (2015a). Master lecture: Inside/outside with trauma survivors. University of San Juan, Puerto Rico, April 30, 2015.

Horovitz, E. G. (2015b). A guided practice: Combining art therapy and yoga therapy for mood management. University of San Juan, Puerto Rico, May 2, 2015.

Horovitz, E. G. (2015c). Common interest community presentation: Family yoga therapy treatment with a bipolar 11-year-old boy. *SYTAR 2015,* Newport Beach, CA, June 4, 2015.

Horovitz, E. G. (2016a). Efficacy, apps, and telehealth: Treatment for a digital age. American Art Therapy Association 47th Annual Meeting, Baltimore, MD, July 9, 2016.

Horovitz, E. G. (2016b). Photography as therapy: Through academic and clinical explorations. In D. E. Gussak and M. L. Rosal (Eds.), *The Wiley handbook of art therapy* (pp. 180–187). Malden, MA: John Wiley & Sons, Ltd.

Horovitz, E. G. (forthcoming). Efficacy, apps, and telehealth: Treatment and ethical issues for a digital age. In A. Di Maria (Ed.), *Exploring ethical dilemmas in art therapy*. New York, NY: Routledge.

Huss, E. (2010). Bedouin women's embroidery as female empowerment: Crafts as culturally embedded expressions within art therapy. In C. H. Moon (Ed.), *Materials and media in art therapy: Critical understandings of diverse artistic vocabularies* (pp. 215–229). New York, NY: Routledge.

Johnson, J. S., & Wilson, J. E. (2005). "It says you really care": Motivational factors of contemporary female handcrafters. *Clothing and Textiles Research Journal, 23*(2), 115–130.

Kramer, E. (1986).The art therapist's third hand: Reflections on art, art therapy, and society at large. *American Journal of Art Therapy, 24*(3), 71–86.

Krauss, D. (1979). Photo therapy course offered at Kent State (edited by B. Zakem). *Photo Therapy Quarterly, 2*(1), 12–13.

Krauss, D. A., & Fryear, J. L. (1983). *Phototherapy in mental health.* Springfield, IL: Charles C. Thomas.

Krupinski, E. A., & Bernard, J. (2014). Review: Standards and guidelines in telemedicine and telehealth. *Healthcare, 2*, 74–93.

Krupinski, E. A., Antoniotti, N., & Burdick, A. (2010). Standards and guidelines development in the American Telemedicine Association. In A. Moumtzoglou & A. Kastania (Eds.), *E-health systems quality and reliability: Models and standards* (pp. 244–252). Hershey, NY: Medical Information Reference Science.

McNiff, S. (1998). *Art-based research.* Philadelphia, PA: Jessica Kingsley Publishers.

Malchiodi, C. (2012a, February 29). Art therapy: There's an app for that. *Psychology Today*. Retrieved November 1, 2016 from www.psychologytoday.com/blog/arts-and-health/201202/art-therapy-there-s-app.

Malchiodi, C. (2012b, October 31). Cool art therapy intervention #1: The art therapist's third hand. *Psychology Today*. Retrieved July 9, 2016 from www.psychologytoday.com/blog/arts-and-health/201010/cool-art-therapy-intervention-1-the-art-therapist-s-third-hand.

Mitchell, A., & Mitchell, K. (2003). *Liquid polymer clay*. Iowa, WI: Krause Publications.

Moxley, D. P., Feen-Calligan, H. R., Washington, O. G. M., & Garriott, L. (2011). Quilting in self-efficacy group work with older African American women leaving homelessness. *Art Therapy: Journal of the American Art Therapy Association, 28*(3), 113–122.

OCDLA. (n.d.). Trichotillomania: Symptoms and treatment. Retrieved October 28, 2016 from http://www.ocdla.com/trichotillomania.html.

Pavelka, L. (2002). *Polymer clay extravaganza.* Cincinnati, OH: Northern Light Books.

Reynolds, F. (1999). Cognitive behavioral counseling of unresolved grief through the therapeutic adjunct of tapestry making. *The Arts in Psychotherapy, 26*(3), 165–171.

Reynolds, F. (2000). Managing depression though needlecraft creative activities: A qualitative study. *The Arts in Psychotherapy, 27*(2), 107–114.

Reynolds, F. (2002). Symbolic aspects of coping with chronic illness through textile arts. *The Arts in Psychotherapy, 29*, 99–106.

Stathis, M. (2013). Personal communication, Rochester, NY.

Stross, R. (2011, July 9). The therapist will see you now, via the Web. *The New York Times*.

Retrieved September 1, 2015 from www.nytimes.com/2011/07/10/technology/bringing-therapists-to-patients-via- the-web.html.
Weiser, J. (1993). *Phototherapy techniques.* San Francisco, CA: Jossey-Bass Publishers.
Winebrenner, C. (2004). Art behind bars. *Fiberarts, 30*(4), 16.
Winnicott, D. W. (1953). Transitional objects and transitional phenomena: A study of the first not-me possession. *International Journal of Psychoanalysis, 34*, 89–97.
Yarborough, T. (2005). *Surviving twice: Amerasian children of the Vietnam war.* Dulles, VA: Potomac Books.
Yellowlees, P., Shore, J., & Roberts, L. (2010). Practice guidelines for videoconferencing-based telemental health. *Telemedicine and e-Health*, December, *16*(10), 1074–1089.

Websites

Atomic Learning: www.atomiclearning.com (Retrieved June 24, 2017).
BetterWorld Healthcare: www.betterworldhealthcare.com/ (Retrieved December 5, 2016).
Breakthrough: http://drellenghorovitz.breakthrough.com (Retrieved October 13, 2016).
Con Tus Manos: http://fabicontusmanos.blogspot.co.uk/2009/09 (Retrieved October 20, 2016).
Cre8it: www.cre8it.com (Retrieved July 5, 2017).
Delphi: www.delphiglass.com (Retrieved July 5, 2017).
Dharma Trading Co.: www.dharmatrading.com (Retrieved October 13, 2016).
Gimp: www.gimp.org/downloads/ (Retrieved July 28, 2016).
Jacquard SolarFast Negative Generator: www.jacquardsolarfast.com (Retrieved June 9, 2017).
Pinterest (needle and wet felting): www.pinterest.com/simocallioni/needle-and-wet-felting (Retrieved October 20, 2016).
Polymer Clay Web: www.polymerclayweb.com (Retrieved July 18, 2016).
Sculpey: www.sculpey.com (Retrieved July 18, 2016).
SolarFast: https://vimeo.com/72210081 (Retrieved July 18, 2016).

5 Byproducts and Miscellaneous Applications

Our customs, behaviors and values are byproducts of our culture.

Jacque Fresco, "Resource-Based Economy" (n.d.)

Introduction

Artists continually see the beauty in everything, from the colors of their palettes to the remnants of the artistic process. Artistic souls very often find that the beauty of discarded products can be more alluring than the original output. So beyond the obvious measure of scanning the digital work back into the computer and manipulating cast-offs via software (Horovitz, 2011), I began taking byproduct art to new heights and recycling products that would otherwise be composted or thrown out. And I frequently preferred the byproduct to the original intended outcome. So in this chapter, I will describe some of the techniques that I use, sometimes in combination with the original intended result, and other times as an entity in and of itself.

I am not sure if it was my vegetable garden, my compost pile, or just the allure of my essential oils, but for whatever reason, one day, I decided to take my recycling of natural products a step further. I have always repurposed things and composted. One of my favorite books that got me started was a little gem called *Let it Rot! The Gardener's Guide to Composting* (Campbell, 1975), followed by another called *Grow Your Own: An Introduction to Organic Gardening* (Darlington, 1970). I read these in the 1970s, and they changed my life and how I viewed the world. It took several years later for me to realize that byproducts from my garden might invade my studio in the form of soap making, eco-dyeing, gourd birdhouses, aluminum cans, and more. Byproducts of existing art products were covered in depth in my 2011 book, using cast-offs from my digital output and transforming them; rather than repeat those concepts in this book, I am going to focus more on byproducts from available materials (read: not digitized) in your nearest garden, recycling bin, etc.

Making Soap

One day, I decided to make my own soap. Basically, you take oils, which make you greasy, and turn them into soap, which makes you clean. This process is called saponification (making soap). Soap is really a science, and I love science. Once you select the oils and mix them with sodium hydroxide (lye) and a liquid, the molecules combine, a chemical reaction occurs (saponification), and a totally different substance is created: soap!

The Cold-Process Method

While you can actually make soap from scratch, many people are put off the idea because you have to use the ingredient lye, which is caustic. Natural does *not* mean chemical-free, because you cannot make soap without lye. It's a good idea to have vinegar around (just in case the lye comes in contact with your skin) because you do *not* want to put water on the lye that has come in contact with the skin, only vinegar! Always be extra careful when using lye. When you mix the lye with your liquid materials, it will heat up and fume for about 30 seconds to a minute. *A well-ventilated area is a must.* Even though lye is caustic and dangerous to work with, after it reacts with the oils in your soap, no lye will remain in your finished soap. *Gloves and eye protection are a must!* And for clean-up, I fill the sink with some vinegar just in case there are any mishaps. *Always* add lye to water (*not* water to lye) and start stirring right away. If allowed to clump on the bottom, it could heat up all at once and cause an explosion. For these reasons, many purchase soap that is already prepared (premade melt-and-pour soaps), with only the need to heat and add your own homemade elements. This will be covered further on in this section.

However, for those who are more adventurous, I will offer recipes below and there are also excellent videos on YouTube that will walk you through this very easy process of making soap from scratch – for instance: "Super Easy Soap for Beginners" (www.youtube.com/watch?v=qGfXLznJJY0), "Handmade Cold Process Soap Coming to a Trace Olive Oil Castile Soap Shown" (www.youtube.com/watch?v=YKBUwV_AbYw), or "How to Make Cold Process Soap" (www.youtube.com/watch?v=yR6ttCSrLJI).

Again, if you do not want to make your own soap, you can purchase melt-and-pour soap on the open market from your local craft store or at various places such as Bulk Apothecary (www.bulkapothecary.com) or Bramble Berry (www.brambleberry.com). So, I offer you guidance on how to make both types of soap so you can choose which method you would prefer to use for your practice. While some art therapists may choose to only use the melt-and-pour soaps available on the open market, on your own, you might want to experiment with the cold-process method.

Benefits

- If you can follow a recipe, you can make cold-process soap.
- You can make products that are hand made and with artistic quality.

- Products made using the cold-process method last longer than other types of soap and can be tailored to benefit people with skin conditions.

Cold-Process Soaps: Guidelines

The process involves dissolving lye (sodium hydroxide) in liquid (most often water, tea, frozen goat's milk, etc.). The lye–liquid solution is then added to melted oils (coconut oil, palm oil, or lard).

Working with lye requires some care because of the strong fumes and risk of burning the skin, but overall it is an easy process that allows you the benefit of controlling exactly what goes into your soap. You can add coloring, fragrance, herbs, exotic oils, and butter – anything you like. The soap is poured into silicone or wooden molds for larger batches (later cut) and needs to cure for three to six weeks.

Time Required

Soap is made in a two-step process: making the soap, then unmolding and cutting for curing. This can take a few hours, so it is best to have a half a day or a whole evening.

Skill Level and Soap-Making Instructions

You need to follow the directions to set up. You need to understand and use safety precautions when handling lye. *Always wear safety goggles, long-sleeved shirts, rubber gloves, and long pants! Be in a well-ventilated area! Avoid any contact with eyes (thus the need for safety glasses).* If you do get lye in your eye, flush for 15 minutes with water. If you get it on your skin, it is better to flush it with vinegar.

Product

Soap will require three to six weeks to cure; you need to plan this out if you or your patient wishes to gift soap to family and friends. The process allows you to perfect your own signature soaps.

Where to Buy Soap-Making Supplies

General supplies can be bought at the grocery store; lye can be bought at the hardware store. You may need to look into soap-making suppliers for certain oils and additives (I highly recommend Bramble Berry: www.brambleberry.com).

Basic Cold-Process Recipe: 5% Superfat

Ingredients

- 8 oz coconut oil (33%)
- 8 oz olive oil (33%)
- 8 oz palm oil (33%)
- 7.9 oz distilled water
- 3.4 oz lye (sodium hydroxide).

Supplies Needed

- Heat-safe, non-reactive containers and utensils
- Immersion stick blender.

Instructions

This recipe is composed of coconut oil, olive oil, and palm oil. These three oils are some of the most common in soap making, and all offer something different to hand-made soap. Coconut oil and palm oil both give the soap firmness. Olive oil gives soap a mild and creamy lather. Coconut oil is very cleansing in nature and gives the soap a large lather. A very common soap recipe is 33% coconut oil, 33% olive oil, and 33% palm oil. Some people feel that soap containing more than 25–30% coconut oil is drying. This is a personal preference, but this recipe was formulated to accommodate sensitive skins. The proportion of olive oil was increased to ensure that the bars are gentle. This recipe contains 5% superfat. This means that 5% of the oils in this recipe are not turned into soap, and are free-floating in the soap. In other words, this recipe contains 5% less lye than necessary to turn 100% of the oils into soap. (Every oil has a saponification (SAP) value.) You need to calculate how much lye it will take to saponify or turn into soap. For example, how many grams of lye will it take to turn how many grams of oil into soap? Fortunately, there is a calculator and an app for that! See Bramble Berry's lye calculator at: www.brambleberry.com/Pages/Lye-Calculator.aspx.

If you change out your oils, you have to recalculate the SAP value or you might ruin your next batch of soap, since each oil has its own SAP value.

Type of oil	*Weight*	*SAP Value*
Olive oil	8 oz	.134
Coconut oil	8 oz	.190
Palm oil	8 oz	.141

1 *Always* add your lye to water, *not* the other way around! It heats up and you want to let it cool down. *Never use aluminum.* Always use a stainless steel, glass, or wooden spatula; be sure to use a heat-safe, non-reactive container (glass or plastic) and utensils when mixing lye!
2 After the lye is mixed, let it cool to 145 degrees Fahrenheit (you can use a candy thermometer for this but there are digital thermometers available as well). Then, slowly heat the combined oils to around 135 degrees Fahrenheit. Slowly add the lye–water mixture into the oils and mix together until it traces (forms little lines and indentations on top of the mixture). Use a stick immersion tool to do this. *(Hint: Tracing the oil is when the lye–water mixture and the oils stick together to make soap.)*
3 Next, you can add fragrance or essential oil. Then, pour the mixture into the molds, wrap the soap in a towel, and leave it for 24 hours. After popping the soap out of the molds, you need to wait four to six weeks before using or gifting. Place the soap in a cool area and rotate it (on all of its sides) over the next four to six weeks. When using fragrances, use between 0.7 oz and 1 oz of fragrance oil to 1 lb of soap. This helps avoid acceleration, ricing, or seizing in the final product.

The Melt-and-Pour Method

Many people, especially beginners, prefer to buy premade soap bases instead of starting from scratch. These soap bases, often called glycerin soaps, can be found in most craft stores. If you are interested in purchasing organic or specific bases using less common oils, your best bet is to purchase online with soap-making suppliers such as Soap Queen (www.soapqueen.com) or Bulk Apothecary (www.bulkapothecary.com).

Benefits

- This method has an easy, fast set-up and a quick clean-up.
- You do not need to use lye.
- It is versatile and creative, so you can make it personal.
- The product is ready within an hour of setting up and becoming a solid; this is the method to use if your patient needs something more immediate than the cold-process soaps mentioned above.

Melt-and-Pour Soaps: Guidelines

This method consists of using premade soap products or ready-made blocks (goat's milk, olive oil, glycerin) and melting them in the microwave or double boilers.

Once the soap base is hot and liquid, you can then add color (dyes or natural colorants), scent (fragrance or essential oils), and even exfoliating ingredients (such as oatmeal or dried herbs) as well as butters and oils (jojoba oil, Vitamin E, or buttermilk) to soften and smooth the skin.

Once the mixture has been poured into the molds (candy molds, plastic dishes and containers, or purchased soap molds) and allowed to set, the result is usable soaps. (I prefer silicone molds and use Wilton bake molds since the soap pops out with ease and the styles available are gorgeous.)

Time Required

Soap can be made in about 60 to 90 minutes.

Skill Level and Soap-Making Instructions

Anyone can do it, so this works for all populations. (Obviously, since you are working with heated soap, care needs to be taken when working with small children.)

Product

Soap is ready right away and you can be very creative with this method, especially if you have access to fun molds.

Where to Buy Soap-Making Supplies

The craft store and your own kitchen equipment should be enough.

Basic Melt-and-Pour Recipe: Oatmeal and Honey

Ingredients

- 454 grams (1 lb) of melt-and-pour soap base
- ¼ cup coarsely ground rolled oats
- 1 tsp honey
- 3 tsp essential oils or fragrance.

Supplies Needed

- Sharp knife
- Cutting board
- Glass measuring cup
- Measuring spoons

- Mixing spoons and wood stirrers
- Spray bottle (small) with rubbing alcohol
- Rubber spatula
- Molds (I love silicone bakeware, but you can use metal baking pans, candy or candle molds, and/or plastic containers)
- Plastic wrap or airtight containers (I use clear cellophane wrap on my soaps).

Instructions

You will be heating your premade soap base in a double boiler or the microwave. Make sure that your molds are prepared. I like to place my molds onto a tray so that if I need to move the soaps, I don't disrupt the molds themselves (Figure 5.1). If you are adding items like toys, as shown in Figures 5.1 and 5.2, you will need to add just a bit of soap to the bottom of the mold and then press the toy or object into the bit of glycerin soap. That way, the toy does not float as the soap fills the mold contents.

1. Measure out your color, additives, and scents (essential or fragrance oils).
2. Cut the premade soap base into small chunks using the knife.
3. Heat the chunks in the double boiler with the lid on over a medium heat, or place them in the glass measuring cup and heat them in the microwave, using 20-second increments and stirring in between.
4. When melted, stir in color, additives, and scents.
5. Pour into the mold(s).
6. *Very important*: Spray the top of the soap with rubbing alcohol to remove any air bubbles.
7. Allow the soap to harden. It can take 1 to 12 hours.
8. Pop the soap out of the mold(s). You may want to put the soap in the refrigerator for ten minutes to make it easier to remove from your molds.
9. Wrap the soap in plastic wrap or cellophane, or place it in an airtight container.

Coloring Soap Naturally

Natural colorants result in much softer and more muted colors than those you may be used to seeing in commercial soaps, which usually use artificial colors in their manufacture. While some natural colorants give you only color, others give you more, such as exfoliation, antioxidants, or other benefits. Below is a list from Debra Maslowski at DIY Natural (2014) of some colors that she has produced from natural ingredients, which also includes some of the added benefits of each ingredient. Also remember that the color of your base soap will interact with the colors that you add! You can also add flower petals for color.

Figure 5.1 Top: (left to right) A silicone mold with toys; essential oils and lavender oil; a cutting board with lavender, flower petals, oatmeal, rosemary leaves, and a knife. Bottom left: A toy adhered to soap. Bottom right: The finished product, with the toy surrounded by flower petals, lavender, oatmeal, and other natural elements.

- Alfalfa: (use dried, ground) gives a medium green color
- Alkanet root: (infuse in oil) produces a purple to blue color
- Annatto: (infuse in oil) produces a yellow to orange color
- Beetroot powder: produces a squash yellow color; contains antioxidants
- Black walnut hull: (use dried, ground) adds purple to black specks; exfoliating
- Blue cornmeal: produces a purplish blue to brown color; exfoliating
- Calendula: (dried, whole flowers) produces yellow streaks; has healing properties

Figure 5.2 Top: Finished soaps embedded with toys, natural ingredients, and essential oils. Bottom: Finished soaps embedded with natural ingredients and essential oils.

- Calendula: (powdered) adds a yellow color; has healing benefits
- Carrots: (use ground, raw) produces a yellowish orange color; contains beta carotene
- Chamomile: (use dried, powdered) produces a beige to yellow color
- Chamomile essential oil, German: (also known as blue chamomile) produces a light green color
- Chlorophyll: (use powdered) produces a green color; has deodorizing properties
- Chocolate: (use a melted chocolate bar) produces a brown color
- Cinnamon: produces a brown color; can be irritating to some skin types
- Cloves: (use ground) produces a brown color; can be irritating to some skin types
- Cocoa powder: produces a brown color
- Coffee: (finely ground) produces a brown to black color; exfoliating, has antioxidants, and removes odors
- Coffee: (instant) produces a brown to black color; antioxidant and odor eliminating
- Cornmeal: produces a yellow color; exfoliating
- Elderberries: (use in lye) produces a light brown color; high in antioxidants even though the original color has changed
- Green tea powder: produces a brownish green color; has antioxidants
- Henna: produces an olive green to greenish brown color
- Indigo powder: produces a deep blue color; *caution – stains easily!*
- Kelp: produces a green color; contains minerals and iodine in minute amounts
- Madder root: produces a red to purple color
- Milk: produces shades of beige to brown, maybe orange
- Moroccan red clay: produces a brick red color; draws out impurities in the skin
- Orange juice: (use in place of water in lye–water solution) produces beige to light orange colors; lowers the pH of the soap
- Paprika: produces an orange color
- Poppy seeds: adds black specks; exfoliating
- Pumice: produces a gray color; exfoliating
- Rose hips: (use ground) produces a burgundy to brown color; high in Vitamin C
- Rose-pink clay: produces a brownish pink color; draws out impurities in the skin
- Safflower petals: produces a yellow to orange color
- Saffron: produces a yellow color
- Sage: (use dried, ground) produces green to brown colors
- Sandalwood powder: (depends on the type used) red produces a brownish red color; yellow produces a yellow to beige color
- Spearmint: (use dried, ground) produces a green to brown color
- Spinach: (use dried, ground) produces a light green color

- Spirulina: produces a green to bluish green color
- Tree lichen: (depends on the type used) produces a range of colors from pink to green to brown
- Turmeric: produces a yellow color
- Wheat grass juice: (use dried) produces a green color
- Woad powder: produces blue shades; *caution – can stain!*

You can see that many of the natural items used in soap making are similar to (if not the same as) those used in naturally coloring fabrics or hair. Don't be afraid to experiment, though there are some things that can't or shouldn't be used. For more ideas and great resources, see Faiola (2016) and Ittner (2011). *(N.B.: Always be sure to keep track of your recipes. I keep detailed notes and record each batch, even if I've made it a dozen times before. That way, I can keep each batch consistent or change things, as I like.)*

Population Benefits and Contraindications

As described above, this can be a wonderful medium with immediate results (that is if you choose to make the basic melt-and-pour recipe). The results are extremely tactile and in fact, if the medium is used with a population that struggles with hygiene, having the control of making your own soap products can be quite an incentive for altering that behavior. This would work well with any age population (children need to be monitored closely). T from Chapter 4 (Figure 4.55) would benefit enormously from making his own soap for an increased incentive to bathe more often. I have made soap products with numerous populations and ages and have found that the science of the material's state change (from a liquid to a usable solid) lends an alchemical magic to art therapy. I have not yet discovered a population averse to using this medium and in some instances it has spurred creativity and future cognitive interest in science.

More Ideas from the Garden

Making Eye Pillows

As a certified yoga therapist and licensed art therapist, I often intertwine yoga therapy and art therapy where it is appropriate. In the final relaxation *asana* (pose) during yoga therapy, the patient lies prone on a yoga mat, eyes closed, and is often covered with a yoga blanket. Figure 5.3 shows two cancer survivors from a group that I led for over a year. This all-female group moved from yoga therapy to art therapy, sharing their stories, hopes, disappointments, deaths, and

Figure 5.3 Cancer survivor group members in *savasana* with eye pillows over their eyes.

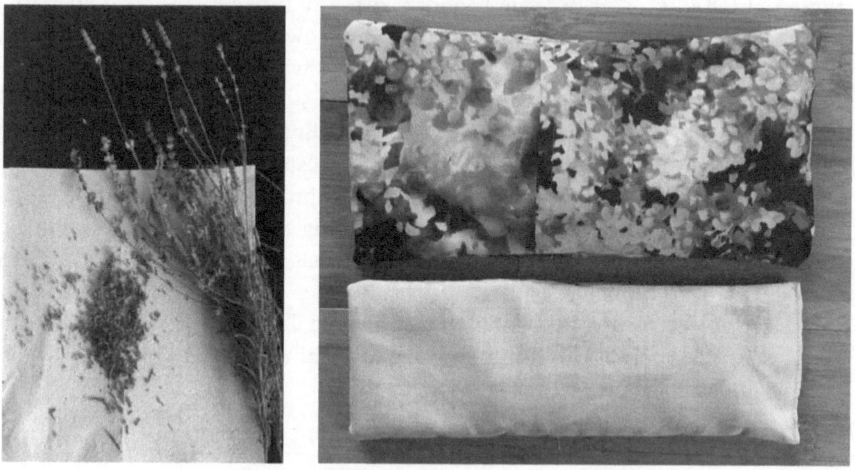

Figure 5.4 Left: A mixture of organic dried lavender and organic flax seeds. Right: A finished lavender eye pillow, comprising an outer layer with floral pattern (above) and an inner pouch (below).

prayers. This image illustrates the restorative properties of that final relaxation state, *savasana*. Figure 5.4 shows an eye pillow that was made for this group from organic harvested lavender dried out and mixed with organic flax seeds for the inner pouch. (The inner pouch can be removed so that the outer layer can be washed for hygienic purposes.) Many of these women liked working in fibers (creating and dyeing their own silk scarves) and fabricating these eye pillows. Used at room temperature or placed in the freezer or microwave, they can have an enormous restorative effect on numerous populations.

Population Benefits and Contraindications

As illustrated, making lavender eye pillows can be extremely therapeutic when used with populations such as cancer survivors. Moreover, these medicinal relaxation items can be used with patients for de-stressing or when experiencing pain such as migraines. I have found these to also benefit my patients with fibromyalgia and various other ailments. The only contraindication might be with patients who have an aversion to specific smells. Overall, I have never experienced any complaints when using these items.

Eco-Dyeing

During my yearlong saunter into quilting with the Fiberistas (previously mentioned in Chapter 4), I became friendly with a number of the women in the group. One of them, Mary, whose artwork is shown in Figure 4.44, began to wonder about eco-dyeing. The idea of working with nature as the source of natural products with which to dye and adorn silk piqued my interest, so I explored this in great depth. After scouring the internet and spending weeks researching, I was able to produce some terrific results using natural mordants, such as vinegar and copper. This resulted in stunning one-of-a-kind products that are easy to do with patients. Like everything else mentioned herein, it is important that you take care in writing down what you have done in the event that you want to replicate your results (as closely as possible). While I used silk for these projects (graciously donated by Dharma Trading Co., www.dharmattrading.com) you can use cotton or other natural fabrics. So let's look at how this is done and, once again, at the science involved.

The Materials and Process of Eco-Dyeing

Water and pH

Water quality is very important in natural dyeing since the results may vary depending on the pH. Clean water will produce more effective colors (which may not be your desired effect) than water with a high iron content. Some plants may change dramatically by changing the pH content. For example, red cabbage in a more acid liquid (e.g., vinegar) will turn violet; in a more alkaline base, it may turn to blue or ocean green.

Fabric Preparation

While some fabrics are prewashed, if not, it is best to start by washing the fabrics to be dyed with Synthrapol or a similar cleaner (Synthrapol is available from Dharma Trading Co.)

Mordants

Mordants are what makes the dye adhere to the fabric. Some natural mordants used in dyeing are alum or potassium aluminum sulfate, cream of tartar, and iron or copper. For example, you can make your own homemade mordants by filling a jar with a few scraps of copper pipe and 50% water and 50% vinegar. In short order, the water will appear blue. The filled jar can be used as a dye bath. Another method of pre-mordanting your fabric is soaking it in a mix of alum dissolved in water. (Use 1 g of alum for every 100 g of silk.) A good rule is to leave the fabric in there for two to three days. You can also mordant the fabric during the eco-dyeing process and not use a pre-mordant (referred to as co-mordanting).

Adding Metal or Byproducts

You can also wrap the fabric around rusted metal (with iron content or copper) to enhance colors and co-mordant behavior. Another method of co-mordant dyeing is to wrap the fabric around a copper pipe after the fabric has been tied together. A simple pipe cutter and copper tubing can be used for this. This is my preferred method of eco-dyeing, using a vinegar/water bather for steaming the fabric (Figure 5.5).

Adding the Plant Material

You can use fresh leaves or flowers, but based on my research, I have found that freezing your flowers, whether from fresh or from a dried bouquet, works better since the frozen petals encourage the dye from the plant to travel into your fibers. Whether adding plant materials or metal byproducts, I lay the fabric out and place the plant materials and metal onto it. Then, I roll the entire thing up from the bottom to the top and tie with twine, string, or rubber bands.

Steaming the Fabric

If you do not have a steamer, you can place the fabric directly in clean water. *(N.B.: Silk loses its luster when boiled so, as can be seen in the bottom image of Figure 5.5, I prefer to steam the fabric.)* For photographic purposes, I uncovered this pot, but you should always keep the pot covered and steam for at least 30 minutes. Let it cool down naturally. Once cool, remove the fabric, still bound, and leave it out to dry naturally for at least two to three days. (It is best to do this when the weather is warm.) It is important that the air can get to the tied bundle so that mold does not grow on the fabric! Sometimes, I leave my fabric tied for at least seven days.

Ironing and Rinsing the Finished Product

After unwrapping the fabric, and removing the leaves, flower petals, and so on, you should iron the silk scarf on the silk setting and let it air dry for another seven days. Finally, you can rinse the scarf with clean water and a tiny bit of Synthrapol, Woolite, or liquid soap detergent. (Figure 5.6 illustrates some finished silk scarves.)

Eco-Dyeing Watercolor Paper

You can replicate this entire process using watercolor paper. You stack the papers together with materials on each page and then wrap with twine. Follow the same process as for eco-dyeing silk scarves.

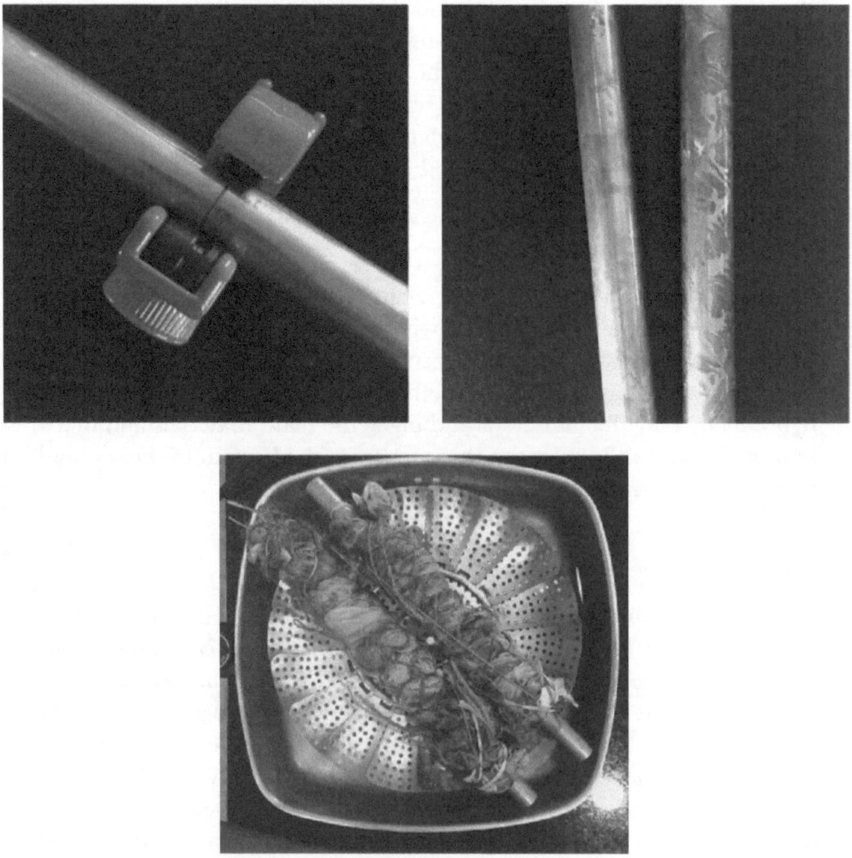

Figure 5.5 Top left: A copper pipe cutter and scored copper tubing. Top right: A vinegar mordant left on copper tubing. Bottom: Silk scarves wrapped and being steamed.

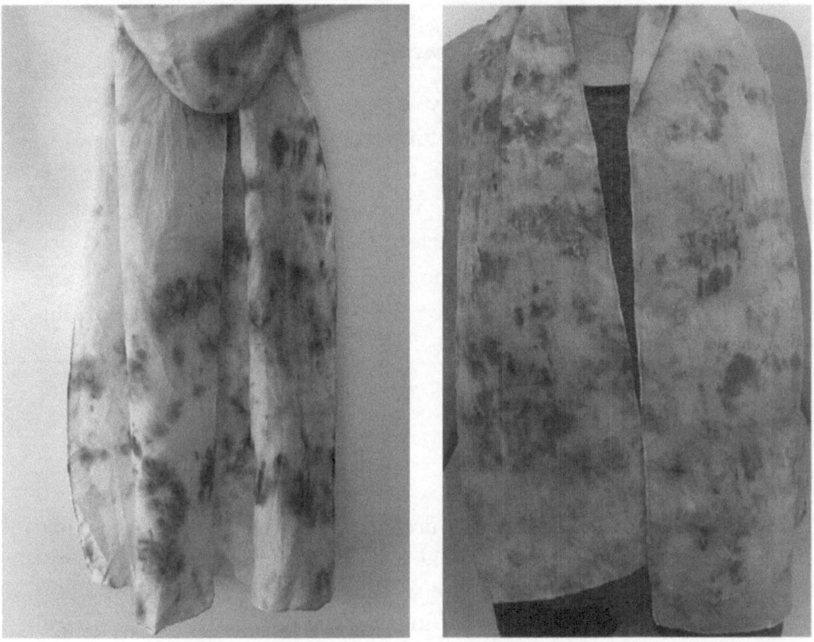

Figure 5.6 Left: A silk scarf after being left to air dry for seven days. Right: A silk scarf made with a mordant of vinegar and copper tubing.

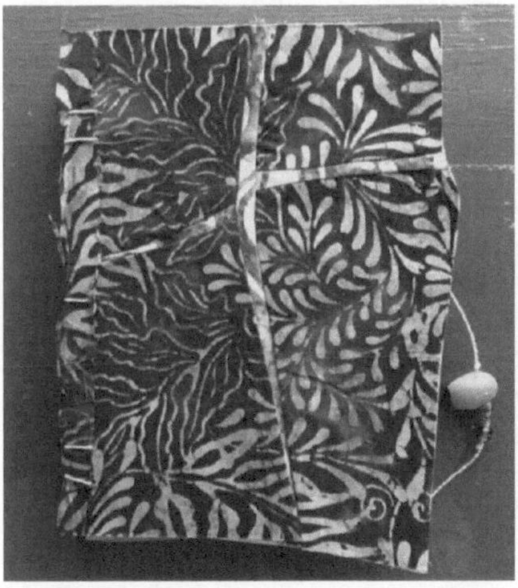

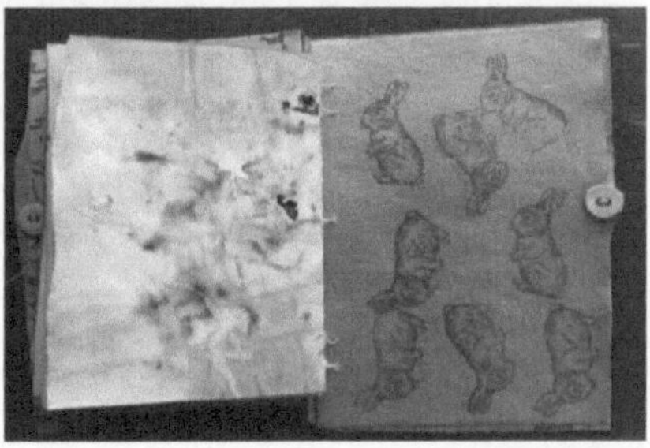

Figure 5.7 The watercolor pages for this journal were eco-dyed and the cover was created by quilting (both created by the author).

Population Benefits and Contraindications

Eco-dyeing is a wonderful activity that can be done outdoors (when nature cooperates) and yields beautiful, wearable art. This can lead to self-esteem in all populations. Obviously, if there are physical ailments that prevent the patient from rolling the scarves, the art therapist can act as a third hand, assisting where directed. The only contraindication (once again) might be with individuals who have extreme constraints regarding impulsivity and frustration tolerance since the final product requires up to a week, or more, for completion.

Gourds and Wood Burning

Fall harvesting is a delight as dried gourds can be transformed into wonderful birdhouses. Using any size drill bit that you wish (Figure 5.8), you can create an opening in the gourd, clean out the seeds (saving them for later should you choose to grow more gourds the following year), and then decorate your gourd however you see fit. I use a 2″ drill bit to open up the gourd and then either carve into the gourd with my wood-burning set and/or decorate/paint it. *(N.B.: You can drill the holes ahead of time so you need not use the drill bit in the session.)* You can also use inks to dye the sides of the gourd should you wish to have more muted and natural colors (see Figure 5.8 for examples). Figure 5.9 shows a wooden bowl that had been discarded for garbage pick-up but was revitalized by a thorough cleaning with Citra Solv and then emblazoned with wood-burning tools.

Population Benefits and Contraindications

Obviously, you should be careful when working with wood-burning tools, choosing your population carefully. But my experience has been exceptionally positive using such materials one on one. In fact, I have even used soldering guns and propane torches with an emotionally disturbed Deaf child without any incident (Horovitz, 2007). So, with an established therapeutic alliance, most tools can yield great gain.

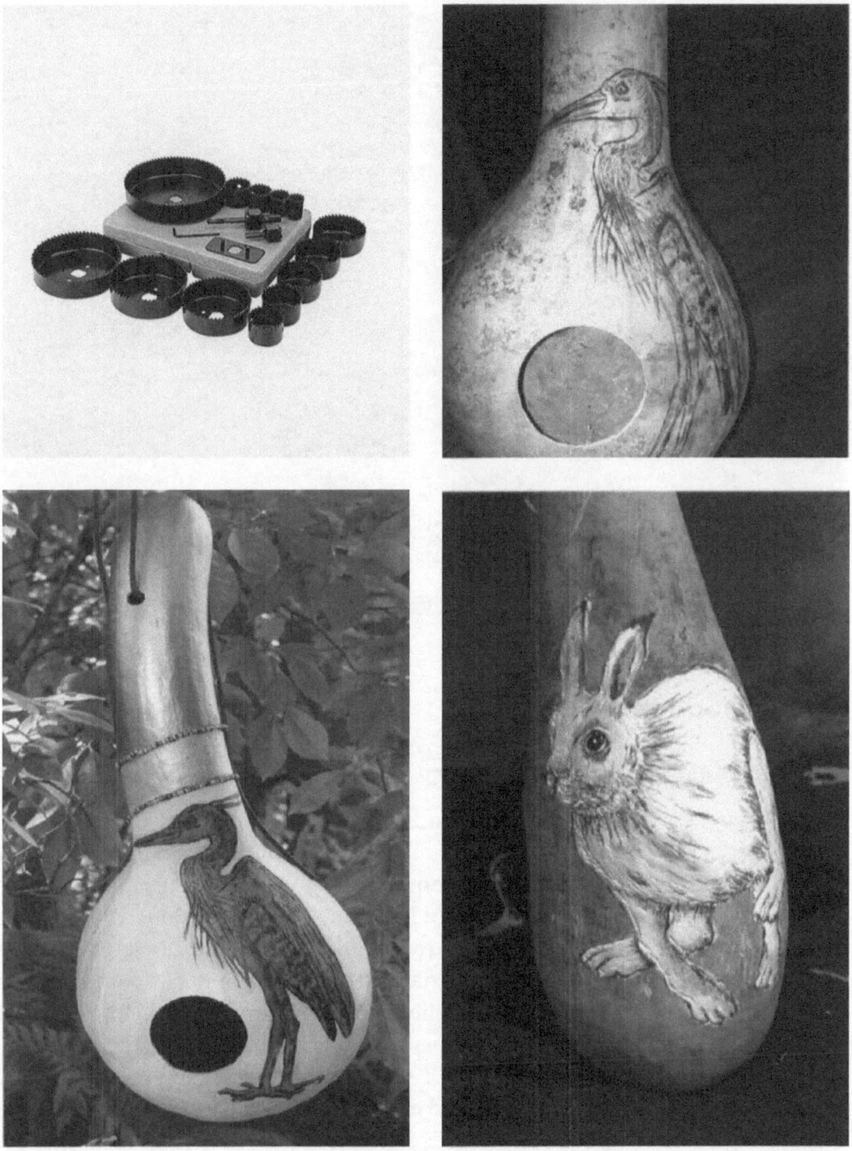

Figure 5.8 Top left: A drill bit set. Top right: An image created by the author using woodburning tools. Bottom left: The final image painted and decorated with beads. Bottom right: Another example created by the author using acrylic paint on a gourd.

Figure 5.9 A discarded wooden bowl that was reclaimed and had cranes burned into it by the author.

Using Found Materials

Making Masks, Casts, and Worry Dolls

I have always scoured the ground for materials to be used in art. On more than one occasion, I have dragged rusted metal, cardboard, bird feathers, and discarded aluminum back to my studio. I have even written about preserving a perfect specimen of a dead fly in order to draft it at a later time (Horovitz, 2005). I have talked to many of my friends who are also artists and we all seem to be attracted not just to discarded materials but to materials that are deteriorated, weathered, and disintegrated. I call this artistic mentality, others might call it a Depression-era mentality (My parents and grandparents lived during that era and their thinking most certainly was passed onto me.) Or perhaps it is just finding beauty even in what others deem unsightly, shabby, and useless. Whatever the reason, I love working with byproducts, cast-offs of previous artwork, and/or materials earmarked for disposal. One of the items I love to work with is cardboard that has been discarded for recycling. It can be reused in the creation of papier-mâché projects (Figures 3.7–3.10) and many other items. In Figure 5.10, a cardboard box has been cut up and repurposed into a mask simply by reconstructing the parts with a glue gun, acrylic paint, and some twine. I took this down to Puerto Rico when I engaged other art therapists (for a lecture/workshop) to create masks from found objects.

I have also used clothespins and found objects to create worry dolls for myself and with patients. Figure 5.11 shows an example of a worry doll clothespin that I created alongside my students. The addition of the "H" (since my students

Figure 5.10 A cardboard mask created for an art therapy workshop by the author.

Figure 5.11 A worry doll created by the author.

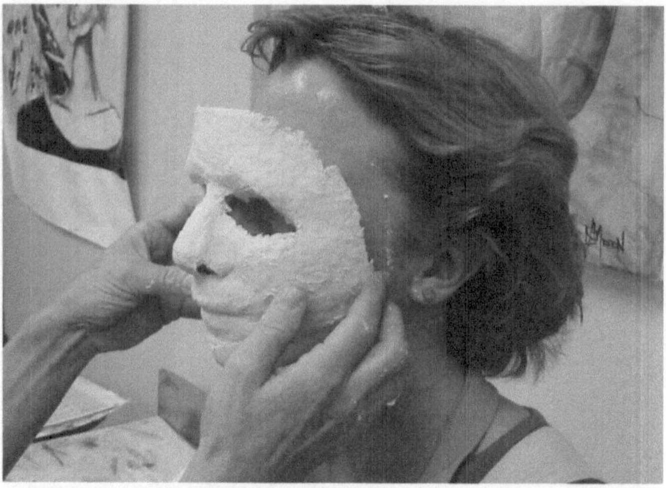

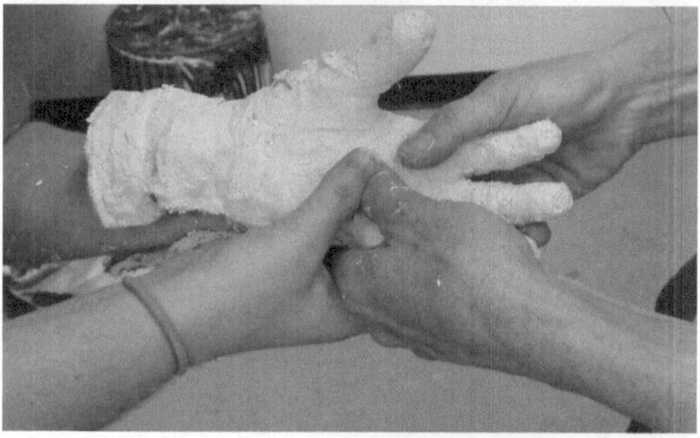

Figure 5.12 Top: A mask created using plaster gauze. Middle: A hand cast created using plaster gauze. Bottom: An image created by an 11-year-old burn survivor.

called me Dr. H) as well as the nail/staff held in the doll's right hand was a direct stand-in for my identity as an artist. Simple as this example was, it spoke volumes to me and every time I saw it, its image made me laugh and worry a lot less.

Another way to create a mask is by using plaster of Paris, a gauze material that is embedded with plaster (how medical doctors immobilize and reset a broken bone). Many doctors and medical supply houses have furnished me with kind donations of such plaster gauze material to use with emotionally disturbed medical patients. I have found it particularly useful to train art therapy students to use plaster gauze since having your face or hand encased into plaster requires great trust that the eventual product can be removed. It's also exceptionally messy. Using Vaseline or a similar release product on whatever is to be cast can bring up feelings of constriction and fear. It is particularly useful to use such materials with patients who have had medical issues.

In Figure 5.12, the top image shows a mask being removed from a student's face, the middle image shows a plaster hand cast being removed, and the bottom image shows an image created by an 11-year-old girl who had been severely burned; the mask was later painted. While this image was *not* created on the young girl's face (but over a template of newspaper covered with plastic), it offered the patient an enormous amount of control to recreate her medical situation in art therapy.

In Chapter 3, Figure 3.32 (W's plaster gauze hands, painted in silver) indicates another use for plaster gauze materials for therapeutic ends. W's decision to paint the hands silver was related to the Tin Man from *The Wizard of Oz*: W wanted his hands to be frozen (like the Tin Man's heart) so that he would not repeat abusing others as he had done in the past. In that same chapter, Figure 3.25 shows two 12-year-old girls engaged in creating a collograph print using discarded cardboard. As can be seen, cardboard can have a multitude of uses when repurposed for another life.

Population Benefits and Contraindications

As described in this section, working with plaster of Paris or plaster-embedded gauze can bring up all kinds of associations from past medical issues to feelings around "good touch"/"bad touch" (for example, when working with a sexually abused patient such as W). However, working through these issues and creating a safe, supportive, and therapeutic environment can counter previously held beliefs around touch and move a patient towards wellness and healing.

Bracelets

Throughout human history, people have adorned themselves with jewelry. While beautiful objects can be fashioned from fine metal, polymer clay (such

Figure 5.13 Bracelets fashioned from byproducts. Left: A bracelet created by a recovering alcoholic woman. Center and right: Jigsaw puzzle bracelets created by the author.

as Iris Mishly's polymer clay alcohol ink jewelry mentioned in Chapter 4), and gems, discarded objects can also yield very interesting results. Figure 5.13 illustrates a bracelet fashioned by a recovering alcoholic woman, and two examples showing how an old jigsaw puzzle can be refashioned into bracelets with stickies, glitter, and acrylic paint.

Population Benefits and Contraindications

Aiding patients in creating items for adornment obviously addresses issues surrounding self-esteem and self-worth. Encouraging self-worth and self-esteem is in fact the building block of ego maturation and health. Rather than looking at these art objects as frivolous, one can measure a patient's self-esteem by his/her reaction of valuing the self and/or gifting these objects to others. Familial issues may come up and, in fact, push the envelope toward well-being and self-acceptance. I have found making items such as these particularly useful with adolescents.

The Byproduct of Love: A Secondary Gain for the Therapist

While this is not the be-all and end-all of what can be made from discarded products, it certainly may whet your appetite and help you think about how to use other products that you might have discarded. It is best to be resourceful not only since art supplies can often be dear, but also because by recycling materials you are truly making a difference in the world. Mentoring that to your patient(s) breeds respect and appreciation. In so doing, you are not only showing that you care for your patient but also for the world, which we inhabit together.

To that end, I would like to add a final figure, Figure 5.14. This shows an alcohol ink image that I sent my patients illustrated in Figure 2.3. I have always

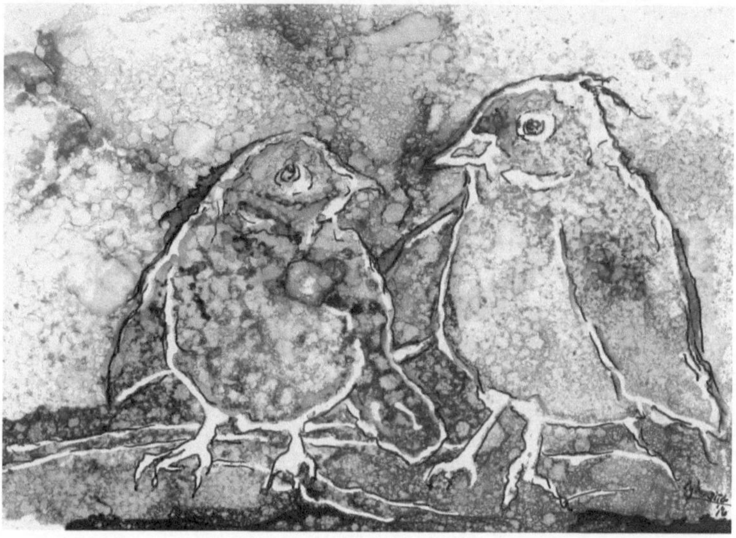

Figure 5.14 A thank you note to my patients: "Birds of a Feather."

said that you need to love your patients. If you do not actually care about them, then you owe it to yourself (and them) to send them to another practitioner. Upon termination, I sent this alcohol ink card, called "Birds of a Feather," to my patients. I thanked them for imparting so much wisdom to me in our two-year period together. While my job was to aid them into physical (and mental) well-being, I received so much more in return from them.

It is a gift to be a part of the healing process. In healing others, you truly do also heal thyself. The old saying from the King James Bible, Luke 4:23, definitely applies here: "And he said unto them, Ye will surely say unto me this proverb, Physician, heal thyself: whatsoever we have heard done in Capernaum, do also here in thy country."

Or, as they say in Latin, "*Medice, cura te ipsum.*"

References

Campbell, S. (1975). *Let it rot!: The gardener's guide to composting.* North Adams, MA: Storey Press.

Darlington, J. (1970). *Grow your own: An introduction to organic gardening.* Berkeley, CA: Bookworks.

Faiola, A. M. (2016). *Pure soapmaking: How to create nourishing, natural skin care soaps.* North Adams, MA: Storey Publishing.

Fresco, J. (n.d.). Resource-based economy: The Venus Project's straightforward approach to the redesign of a culture. Retrieved February 2, 2017 from www.thevenusproject.com/tvphistoryevent/resource-based-economy.

Horovitz, E. G. (2005). *Art therapy as witness: A sacred guide.* Springfield, IL: Charles C. Thomas.

Horovitz, E. G. (Ed.) (2007). *Visually speaking: Art therapy and the Deaf.* Springfield, IL: Charles C. Thomas.

Horovitz, E. G. (2011). *Digital image transfer: Creating art with your photography*. New York, NY: Sterling Publishers.

Ittner, R. (2011). *Soapmaking the natural way: 45 melt-and-pour recipes using herbs, flowers, and essential oils*. New York, NY: Lark Books.

Maslowski, D. (2014, February 21). 44 ways to color soap naturally. *DIY Natural*. Retrieved December 14, 2016 from www.diynatural.com/natural-soap-colorants.

Websites

Bramble Berry: www.brambleberry.com (Retrieved November 25, 2016).

Bulk Apothecary: www.bulkapothecary.com (Retrieved November 25, 2016).

Dharma Trading Co.: www.dharmatrading.com (Retrieved December 6, 2016).

Soap Queen: www.soapqueen.com (Retrieved November 25, 2016).

YouTube, "Super Easy Soap for Beginners": www.youtube.com/watch?v=qGfXLznJJY0 (Retrieved November 25, 2016).

YouTube, "Handmade Cold Process Soap Coming to a Trace Olive Oil Castile Soap Shown": www.youtube.com/watch?v=YKBUw (Retrieved November 25, 2016).

Additional Resources

Art and Craft Safety Guide
https://sis.nlm.nih.gov/enviro/arthazards.html

Citra Solv
www.citrasolv.com

Craftsy
www.craftsy.com

Creative Grids USA
www.creativegridsusa.com

Dharma Trading Co.
www.dharmatrading.com

Dick Blick Art Materials
www.dickblick.com

Genogram Analytics
www.genogramanalytics.com

Gelli Arts
www.gelliarts.com

Glassline Products
www.glasslineproducts.com

Pébéo Art Supplies
www.pebeo.com

PolyPedia Online Express
www.polypediaonlineexpress.com

Roman Decorating Products
http://romandecoratingproducts.com

Sculpey
www.sculpey.com

Slumpy's The Glass Mold Company
www.slumpys.com

Tim Holtz Adirondack Inks
www.timholtz.com

The Warm Company
https://warmcompany.com

Index